HIYA, I'm Nikki, an outspoken, New York loving hun from South Wales, UK, who absolutely adores writing and anything covered in glitter. I am extremely passionate about anything I put my mind to, which can be a huge pain for family and friends (soz, huns). Come laugh with/at me on Instagram @NikkiJMcfarlane

It's a No from Me, Hun

How to Survive all the

Delightful, Crazy Shit Life Throws at You

Nikki J. McFarlane

It's a No from Me, Hun

How to Survive all the

Delightful, Crazy Shit Life Throws at You

Vanguard Press

VANGUARD PAPERBACK

© Copyright 2023
Nikki J. McFarlane

The right of Nikki J. McFarlane to be identified as author of this work has been asserted by her in accordance with the Copyright, Designs and Patents Act 1988.

All Rights Reserved

No reproduction, copy or transmission of this publication may be made without written permission.
No paragraph of this publication may be reproduced, copied or transmitted save with the written permission of the publisher, or in accordance with the provisions of the Copyright Act 1956 (as amended).

Any person who commits any unauthorised act in relation to this publication may be liable to criminal prosecution and civil claims for damages.

A CIP catalogue record for this title is available from the British Library.

ISBN 978 1 80016 833 6

Vanguard Press is an imprint of
Pegasus Elliot Mackenzie Publishers Ltd.
www.pegasuspublishers.com

Although the author and publisher have made every effort to ensure that the information in this book was correct at press time, the author and publisher do not assume and hereby disclaim any liability to any party for any loss, damage, or disruption caused by errors or omissions, whether such errors or omissions result from negligence, accident, or any other cause.

First Published in 2023

Vanguard Press
Sheraton House Castle Park
Cambridge England

Printed & Bound in Great Britain

For my mama, my best friend, my rock. My everything.

For my dad for inspiring me to achieve my dreams. I miss you every single day.

I love you both unconditionally.

Acknowledgements

Mam: I could write a whole other book telling you how thankful I am for you. You are my number one friend and number one supporter. You truly are my rock and the reason I have survived and made it this far. You are the glue that holds us all together and you always add a little extra when we are kicking and screaming to be unstuck and for that I am eternally grateful. You taught me how to be strong but I will always be stronger when I'm with you. You taught me that everything happens for a reason. You taught me to let go of the past and not let others drag me down. You taught me how to be myself and how to dial it down when needed (still working on that). You truly are my everything and I love you more than words can say. Thank you for being you! We did it, Mam!

Dad, I'm thankful that I got to spend twenty-eight years of my life with you. A million wouldn't have been enough. We drove each other crazy but I know you loved me more than anything. Everything I have achieved since you've been gone was to make you proud. I do it for myself but I also do it for you. You inspire me to want to be the most successful person I could possibly be. I love you, Dad!

Demi and Ashton — My two monkeys. The reason I wake up every day and the reason I strive for success. I love you both more than you will ever know. Your hugs and kisses are moments I'll treasure forever, along with all the times you make me act like I'm five. Thank you for unknowingly getting me through tough times and allowing me to love unconditionally. Always fight for what you believe in and never give up on your dreams.

Trina: Thank you for being a great big sister and for all the great memories we share. You unknowingly push me to be a better person than I was yesterday. Even though we don't say it much, I do love you millions.

Celyn: Hun, where do we even begin? Without you I would be locked in a padded cell for life. We were definitely separated at birth even though we were born ten years apart. Our voice note convos have got me through some super shit days. You calm me down, hype me up, and everything in between.

Kirstie: For getting me through the hardest three years of my entire life and for believing in me when I didn't always believe in myself. You are sunshine in human form and I will be forever grateful for you.

Louise: Without you, this book would not be possible. You gave me the idea and kept me in check. You are my muse, ha, ha. You've seen me at my best and at my worst and you have still stuck around. Thank you for always reminding me to believe in myself.

Hannah: For someone I only know through Instagram you are the most amazing friend anyone could ask for. You are the most beautiful soul, have the best sense of humour, and are an absolute babe. You inspire me every single day and always remind me to never settle. Everyone needs a Hannah in their life.

Each and every one of you have made me into the person I am today and for that I thank you a million times over.

Thank you to my amazing publishers, who have made my dreams come true.

And finally, I would like to thank YOU! Thank you so much for reading my book, my blogs, my silly posts, videos, all of it. I really hope you enjoyed reading it as much as I enjoyed writing it. I am truly thankful and grateful to each and every single one of you for buying it. See you in the next one!

Hiya huns,

Survival: a word used often, mainly as a positive and in my case used many, many times to get me through the day.

Now, I don't know about you, and I am certainly not one for dramatics as you will find out as we go along, but I find everyday life a huge ordeal at times. Paying the bills, going to work, ordering a coffee, doing the weekly shop, putting the bins out, smiling to Susan across the street through gritted teeth…the list just goes on and on.

For as long as I can remember, and probably from the day I was born if I could remember that — also a huge ordeal from what my mum says (see where I get my dramatics from) — life has been tough. Now, I am not talking huge life milestones, yes, we all know moving house is the hardest thing in the world blah blah. I am talking everyday mundane tasks or events that we simply must do (but, why?). Apparently, it is what being an adult is. I would like to read through the contract, as I do not recall signing up for this.

Survival is what keeps us going every day. Trying to stay awake all day and be productive on only two hours' sleep is survival. Picking up that Christmas turkey from M&S when they have just told you they are running out, is survival. Asking Alexa to play a song and she gets all defensive and says she doesn't know it. Survival.

I could go on and on and quite frankly I will as otherwise the book would be ending here. Now I am no professional, but I am pretty sure a book needs to be more than half an A4 page. Oooooh, I have another, me reaching the end of this book so I can share all my delightful thoughts with you, yep you guessed it. Survival. I also really had to resist the urge to write 'it's a no from me, hun, just don't do it' for each chapter, but sadly that book would have truly sucked and let's be honest that is just terrible advice, even from me. My survival skills are just impeccable, and they needed to be shared. You are welcome, huns.

Come join me on this fabulous, unfabulous journey where we (we being myself and you, the delightful reader) will put a hilarious spin on your typical mundane tasks, and do and say all the things you're definitely not supposed too…!

Before we delve deep into these life survival skills so great Bear Grylls will be trembling in his (probably made from twigs) boots, please read the below legal disclaimer.

Disclaimer

I have no expert knowledge on how to survive life or any daily life activity. I do not, nor have ever, claim to be a life guru (maybe once or twice after a few gins, but who hasn't?). These opinions are my own and I have not been influenced in anyway. Influencers, back it up! I do believe, however, that this book will help you to survive life. I also do not believe that it will help you survive life nor do I claim any responsibility for any lives not fulfilled by said book.

You will not find me in the woods or drinking my own pee. If you're looking for that kind of book, please refer back to my earlier comment on Bear Grylls. He is the man in the know for any pee drinking related survival tips.

Alcohol may sometimes come up throughout this book (although I am fully teetotal for now and very smug about it). I do not condone it nor am I against it. Drink responsibly and all that jazz.

Please do not take this book camping. It will offer zero help or assistance other than to possibly swat away a few flies. I do not recommend this if viewing on a kindle.

Please note if I were to write an actual survival skills book we would all be eaten by a bear in the first chapter (read first sentence).

I have absolutely no idea what I am doing in life and I am just as fed up as the rest of the world. So, with that being said, let's learn some very high-end life survival skills.

Side disclaimer: You will hear me refer to a number of names throughout this book. These people do not exist other than Carol who is my mama, my bestie and my muse for all the stupid shit I do. She is the best person on Earth and should really have her own chapter. She doesn't but she should. The thought was there.

Dating

'Can I ask you a question?'

'Sure,' I say as I mutter, 'What fresh hell is this dude going to come up with next.'

'If you were the middleman in a human centipede who would you want either end?'

What the actual fuck! Is this what dating is now? Trying to find someone who you don't want to block and run away from on the third question they ask? The audacity.

I am sorry but even if I had been married for ten years to a man I absolutely adored and *he* came out with that question we would be heading to the divorce lawyer pronto. Grow up, you sick son of a bitch.

Dating in general is just a freaking minefield and sometimes I don't think it's worth even dipping a toe into the dating pool. I am just going to sit in my house every day hoping some hottie will knock on my door and whisk me off my feet. Maybe I should leave some shoes lying around; it seemed to work for Cinderella. Although the only shoes you see lying around here are hanging from a tree or electric wire with some poor bastard walking home shoeless. I always wonder how people get themselves into that situation but who am I to judge, I pissed in a potty for F sakes. Bet you can't wait to get to that chapter.

I have also watched waaaaaaay too many thrillers to actually trust anyone. There are so many situations where you could be murdered. Am I about to put myself straight into one of those just to meet a guy? I don't think so, huns. He can keep his murdering self away from me.

Some people love dating but I am just not one of them. I absolutely hate it. Who wants to sit there, date after date asking or being asked the same questions. *Or* not being asked any questions because they are too busy watching darts on the TV screen behind you. Shit sport. Shit guy. Shit date.

I just want to meet someone and for him to sweep me off my feet and to feel fully comfortable from the get go, spend the rest of my life being treated like a queen every day and him coming home from work with a Kate Spade handbag, telling me how beautiful and funny I am. Is that too much to ask, huns? I think not.

I saw a video recently where a woman was writing an invoice for all the men who wasted her time and this chick is an absolute genius. It is not even just the money that was wasted, it is our time. Time is a precious thing and I personally don't want to be spending mine being asked ridiculous questions that tell you nothing about me and are more about you trying to look cool and edgy. When in fact you just look like an absolute dickhead, mate.

Speaking of dicks, no woman I know has ever loved receiving a dick pic so let's just knock that on the head (no pun intended). You may be proud of your penis and I am pleased for you, but I don't want to see it cropping up in my inbox. I have never felt I wanted a man more just because he sent me a pic of his dick. It is an actual turn off for most woman. It isn't pretty, I would rather stick a fork in my eyes. Keep it in your pants and away from my inbox.

Quick story time, I gave my mum my old phone number once, can't remember why, can't remember how. But one day I was sitting minding my own business and Carol screeched. There, sitting in her inbox, was a dick pic. My initial thought was, *Who the hell is sending my married mama their penis*. Then I realised it was my old number and now I was going to have to explain to Carol why I was receiving such photos. Still to this day I have no idea whose penis it was and nor do I wish to know. Carol and I felt completely violated and couldn't go near a hotdog for a good few months. The audacity.

So, it's safe to the say the human centipede man didn't turn out to be my dream man. We went on about five dates. Ha, I'm just kidding, his arse got unmatched immediately and I deleted the whole app not long after that. My poor innocent mind was traumatised.

How to survive dating? Be yourself. Don't take any shit. Always have a friend on standby and if he sends you a dick pic, block him immediately. Your innocent eyes and mind don't need that, huns. Also, people, do not listen to any of my dating advice other than the above as I will probably be single for the rest of my life, surrounded by my Kate Spade handbags. I for one can't wait.

And for those wondering, Gerard Butler and Ryan Reynolds (wink)!

Men

If it really was to rain men, would we be saying Hallelujah? Would we be frolicking in the streets, cheering with glee? I certainly wouldn't be. Hallelujah? You okay, hun? We don't need any more men landing on/in our brains, causing us stress. Trying to duck and dive like I'm in *Mission Impossible* with Tom Cruise. Good grief, hun. It's a no from me. You can keep them, thanks.

Disclaimer before we get into the nitty gritty. This is not about bashing men. I don't hate men, I just think they are stupid arses who do not deserve us. I am fully aware not all men are the same but pretty much most of them act like idiots. We cool? Then off we go...

Me after watching yet another film where the man ends up being an absolute douchebag: 'Urgh, men are such dicks.'

Carol: 'They must realise they are such dicks by now surely. People are on at them all the time about it.'

Oh, how we laughed, but Carol has a fabulous point. Men are constantly doing things that make them absolute bellends. Yet here they are wandering the streets waving their bellends about (metaphorically of course, we hope) like they are the best thing on the planet and yet, we are ones who are hard work…

Oh no, no, no, hun. You just don't fucking listen.

I was balls deep in TikTok one evening (get your minds out of the gutter) and I came across a fabulous woman who just hit the nail on the head with all the stupid shit men say. There was a post about a man saying that if his wife let herself go after they were married and had kids he would basically leave her. The TikTok guru came right back at him and smashed his stupid arse back down.

How very dare you come at us women for 'letting ourselves go' when we've had to deal with your sweaty ball sack and receding hair line even before we were married with kids. (Yes, I'm not married nor do I have kids but I totally bet this is how you feel and I got your back girl.)

It's not even the barbaric shit like that. It's the men thinking we are out here living our lives for them. Most women don't dress for men. We dress for ourselves and other women. We don't wear makeup to impress a man. We wear makeup as it makes us feel good about ourselves. I don't get my nails done to impress a man. I couldn't give two shits if they loved them or hated them. They are for me and to make me feel good.

Let's get one thing straight, us women are a fucking delight and men are lucky to even have one tiny conversation with us never mind spending the rest of their lives on *our* arm. We are the queens and you are just lucky enough to hold our purses and smile.

How to survive men? Just treat them like little puppies. Explain everything to them slowly. Don't take any shit and make sure to send them to the garden when they have been bad. (I would never send an actual puppy out to the garden, they are too precious for that.)

Being a woman in a 'man's world'

Thankfully, we are in 2023 and live in a country where we don't have to ask a man's permission for anything. Yet, we are often treated like the supporting lead rather than the main character. Given that men need us for so many things (ahem, most things) in their lives they don't half try to make it difficult. Where's my equal pay, hun? Why can't you get your own damn keys from your coat where you left them? You know, the important things.

Men sometimes act like we are just a walk on part in their lives. But yep, I am going to say it, without us they would be nothing. *Nothing*, I tell ya.

Back in the olden days (which was only twenty years ago if you ask my niece and nephew. Rude!), women were treated as nothing. We weren't there to have an opinion or even speak unless spoken to. We were there to mother their children, make sure their stomachs were full, and ahem, tend to their needs.

Thankfully we aren't just seen like that any more. We are allowed to have an opinion but only if it is one that a man agrees with. Otherwise, we are told to shush and let the men discuss it.

It blows my mind that there are still so many places of work that are predominantly male and if any woman dares to even think about dipping just a toe into 'their world' all the men are in uproar. A woman working on a building site? Don't talk crazy. Her fragile, little soul couldn't possibly do this — a man's job.

We are freaking awesome and can do any job we want. Don't let men drag you down and get in your brain with silly comments. They are the ones that send unsolicited dick pics, remember? They can't be that bloody smart.

How to survive being a woman in a man's world? We may have to work harder than men, but we are so much stronger than men. Our bodies and minds go through so much, I think we can handle some shitty men with little willy syndrome. Bring it on, babes. We fucking got this!

Huns, read this chapter aloud and proud. Shout it from the rooftops, read it to the men in your lives, read it to strangers in the street. Because you, my babes, are an incredible woman. Own that shit.

Autocorrect/predictive text

Autocorrect will ruin your life faster than any drunken night out will. It is the devil and sometimes I think it is taking the actual piss out of me.

Funny ones are fine. I asked a work colleague to send me some screenshits the other day. That one you can totally laugh at (which I still am doing every time I re-read it, LOL) and carry on.

But my gosh, when the autocorrect is out to get you, there is no laughing, no carrying on. Just staring at the screen in utter disbelief that you've just told your boss you love him and have added some kisses at the end for good measure. *Why does your phone predict kisses for you?* It's not like it's hard to tap the X key a few times. Mind your own business, hun.

Work related autocorrects are the worst. Please let the ground swallow me up when it corrected *how* to *hoe* in a work email. Thankfully I spotted it before I hit that send button. Defo grounds for being fired. I would totally escort myself off the premises after that. Also, I am not sure what that says about me if it changes a normal, everyday word to hoe.

We are so busy and important with our lives you would think we would be welcoming autocorrect with open arms. I don't know about you, huns, but I don't have time (read: I am too lazy) to read over my texts before they get sent, just to make sure the devil that is autocorrect isn't trying to kill me again. I am just not doing it.

Don't even get me started on sending a new man you are chatting too an autocorrect nightmare. That shit will get you blocked quicker than you can say 'it's a no from me, hun'.

Thankfully for my stress levels I don't actually speak with that many people and the ones I do text with we can all have a laugh together about it and no one will be blocking anyone's arse.

I should actually learn from my mistakes and read what I type before I hit that send button, but here we are. I think we've established throughout this book that I am not one to typically learn from any of my mistakes.

Also, whilst we are here, stop correcting it to duck off. I have never ever told anyone to duck off and I doubt I ever will. Pretty sure I am not alone in this. You ducking listening? Urghhh! Uuuuuurgh!

How to survive autocorrect? Pack your things, move to another country, change your name and pretend it didn't happen. Or, if a new identity doesn't seem like an option for you, maybe just laugh, move on and take extra-extra care next time. I'm doing the first option. Ta-ra, huns, ta-ra!

A job interview

Imagine this, you've spent ages tappity tapping away at your computer, applying for all the jobs under the sun. Then, suddenly, you get the phone call. No, you haven't been offered a spot on *Dickinson's Real Deal*, you have made it to the interview stage of the job you applied for.

Insert initial panic as to what job they are actually talking about on the phone as you have applied for so many. You're not really sure what skills you actually have any more and are finding it hard to separate them from the ones that you have elaborated on, or fluffed up, as I like to say.

The dreaded question comes: 'So, what appealed to you about this role?'

Well, given that I cannot remember what company you are even though I have asked you three times, I am not entirely sure this is going to end well. I am going to have to just wing it whilst desperately searching for them on the internet and say, 'I loved that you cover so many things in this role.' Nailed it!

This actually happened to me, and my desperate internet search came up with the wrong company so how I actually made it to a face to face interview and got the job I will never know.

After an awkward/happy phone call come the pre interview jitters. Or in my case, full on panic and anxiety every day until D day. I am such a catch.

Don't get me wrong, getting a job interview is a huge thing to celebrate, especially during particularly challenging times. (Hoping you are reading this in the future and there are dream jobs everywhere for everyone, woohoo.) But ugh, isn't a job interview just the worst, and that's if you even manage to make it that far.

How to survive endless job applications? Grab a gin (or your beverage of choice) a couple of snacks and treat yourself after each one you complete. Or each section if it is one of those stupid long ones that literally ask the same info as I can provide in my CV, thanks, babes.

Planning for an interview is sooooo annoying. I for one hate it. (Don't worry, huns, this book isn't all doom and gloom. Even in the doom and gloom chapters I will add a bit of glitter and sparkles and throw in a crown.) I hate it, but it is a must if you want to nail that interview and show them just how fabulous you are and skilled and experienced for the job, obviously.

How to survive planning for an interview? Get a gin and some snacks…. Oh I see a pattern emerging here. Okay. Ditch the gin and the snacks. Okay. Maybe keep the snacks and the gin but like in the kitchen out of sight or something and just believe in yourself. You got this interview for a reason (unless you pulled a Joey from *Friends* and made up the whole of your CV, in which case I cannot help you) and remember who the fuck you are.

Are we allowed to say fuck? (Insert a more appropriate swear word of choice or just say F if you wish.)

Here we go, strap in, huns, we are off to our interview. The only plus of *whispers* the COVID, was that all interviews were digital and my gosh, what a treat that was. You could be business on the top, party on the bottom. Or in my case ready for bed on the bottom. Comfort is key. PJs are comfy. Enough said.

Digital interviews were such joyous, delightful times. You can have hidden notes at the side. You can fake a dodgy internet connection if you don't know the answer to a question. You can pretend you are going through a tunnel and snap that laptop closed and go about your day. It was an absolute dream. For the record, I never actually did any of those things other than the hidden notes, but my gosh, I would love to be friends with whoever has tried that.

Sadly, pre and post virus, interviews had to be face to face. In a mostly boring, plain room, fully clothed (the horror) with someone firing questions at you. No faking a bad internet connection here, they would probably have you sectioned. 'Nope, sorry, sir, I cannot hear you, have you tried turning your computer off and on again,' whilst he stares at you in disbelief that you could truly be that dumb. I say creative, but there we are.

So, we are all dolled up, preened to within an inch of our lives, prepped like our lives depended on it and are off out the door. If you're anything like me you would have driven the interview route already. Just to keep your anxiety levels down a little. Didn't work. I appear to be gripping the steering wheel like some sort of crazed Grand Prix driver going for the gold. Not entirely sure what the Grand Prix prizes are but you catch my drift.

One big note on surviving an interview is to make sure you do not in any way, from your home to the interview, mess up your outfit. I was in the middle of one once and glanced down to see several holes in the side of my dress. Lovely. Still got the job though. Maybe they saw the holes, thought I needed the cash and took pity on me. This is the same job I later got fired from. So thinking about it now, they definitely did not take pity on me.

Why was I fired, you ask. Well, let's just say they were not very keen on people speaking their minds. Also key to survival, don't speak your mind. But do speak your mind because you are a badass and we need more people who speak out in this world.

How to survive a job interview? Just don't go. Just kidding, I know I said I would resist the urge to say that. Just try and treat it as if your whole life doesn't depend on it and you won't lose your house and three kids (that you definitely do not have) if you don't get it. Simple! But seriously, remember who the fuck you are. Show up and knock them dead.

First day in a new job

Full of high expectations, excitement, hope, nerves and the major anxiety of finding a parking space. It's the first day of a new job and if I don't get there soon I will be turning around and getting back into my PJs. Who needs to pay bills, right?

Not knowing what to really expect is not something I am truly comfortable with. What time am I going to lunch? Can I go pee when I want? Will there be snacks? Do I provide my own snacks? How do I turn this thing on? Like seriously, where is the on button?

Personally, a first day at a new job to me always feels like a first day at my first ever job. I literally lose all of my brain power and act as if I have never left the house before. You want to make a great first impression. You want to show your personality just enough so that your new work besties know you have one, but not so much that they see you are clinically insane and should be sectioned, not turning up to work grinning like a Cheshire cat.

I was late on my first day at one of my jobs and I full on thought I was going to be fired there on the spot. It was a thirty minute drive and I left with one hour and thirty minutes to get there, but apparently the devil was trying to kill me that day and thought it would be great to have roads and lanes closed and make it hell. Thankfully they were amazing and understanding and I was never late again. I was so tempted to buy a house or a patch of land so I could camp right outside to guarantee this would never happen again but felt that was a tad dramatic on my part.

Meeting new people can be super scary but meeting new work people who you may have to see every day is on another level. Will they like me? A hundred percent, duhh. Will I like them? Probably not knowing me. Will they wind me up every single day and make me wish I had stayed in my other job? Almost a hundred percent sure on this one.

Having to slap on a smile and keep it there until five p.m. is bloody hard. Don't get me wrong, you will always meet amazing people who will make you smile naturally. Yet having to keep smiling so they know you are having the best time and be glad they hired you is exhausting. I always want to fast forward to a few months in where they know I am a whiney miserable bitch and I can just get on with my job and be myself. This is often the point where they probably regret hiring me, but try and fire me now, bitches!

How to survive your first day in a new job? Try and win the lottery the night before so you don't have to go. If, and that's a big if, if that fails be as prepared as possible. Plan your outfit the night before. Make sure you have a notebook and two pens. (You don't want to be that person asking for a pen because yours has run out after one sentence.) Take lunch with you and something simple like a sandwich. You don't know what the lunch situation is going to be like. There may be a canteen or a shop nearby but you may also be working in the middle of nowhere. You can't start your first day kicking off with your new work colleagues because you are hangry. And the best advice for pretty much everything, be yourself, as yourself is amazing; unless you are a psychopath, then definitely do not be yourself.

Work/job

Apparently when you are an adult you have to participate in this thing called a job. Now I don't know whose idea this was or what the actual fuck they were thinking but here we are. I didn't ask to be born and now I have to work to survive. What kind of sorcery is this?

Once we get over the initial shock of having to get an actual job (rude, finding a job you really like can be pretty much out of the question). But if you are lucky enough to love your job, it doesn't mean you don't ever want to leave for the day and want to stay at the office twenty-four-seven.

Liking your job but still wanting to finish on time and look forward to weekends and time off is perfectly fine. Just because I run out of the door at five p.m., it doesn't mean I hate my job. I don't have to work overtime to show how much I love my job. You pay me nine to five, I will work nine to five. Obviously if there is a drama etcetera I won't just be out the door leaving a trail of dust like superman. Ta-ra, huns, ta-ra. Good luck with that shit hitting the fan over there. Have a good weekend, see you Monday.

It is the same with answering work messages or emails outside of work hours. Not doing this does not mean you don't care about your job. Also doing this does not mean you are some kind of saint and deserve a gold medal.

Having our work emails on our phones at our fingertips is so dangerous. We will all be guilty of having a sneaky peak. I used to look at my emails and messages on Sunday night to prepare myself for Monday. I didn't do anything with them until Monday but I felt like I needed to know what was awaiting me at nine a.m. the next day. I then found this was stupid and I was wasting my Sunday evening and getting into work mode when I was still in rest mode. Plus, if it was an annoying email I would be pissed off all night thinking about it.

Being busy at work does not mean you do not take your entitled breaks. It may just mean structuring your day better to make time for them. Or, working through a lunch, but making sure it doesn't happen all the time.

We've all been there, super busy at work with no time to pee, never mind take a lunch break. It is soooo important to take your breaks. Not taking lunch breaks doesn't make you amazing, it makes you stupid and it sets up the working place to become a toxic space. New people start, they see you doing the same and they follow suit because they think it is expected of them. Set a good example and stop it.

Taking time away makes you more productive and better at your job. Working all the hours without breaks doesn't make you better at the job. You will find it will burn you out, you'll start making silly mistakes and it can even have an impact on your personal life and mental health.

This got me thinking about high paying jobs where you are expected to work until two a.m. and back in for six a.m. the next day. You hear people saying ah yes, but they get paid mega bucks for this. Umm no, they get paid for their working hours just like everyone else. They get paid for how important and how much responsibility the job requires. Overtime is just that, overtime that you are getting paid for. Now shut that laptop down, babes, and go to the pub or something. The stocks will fall if you are watching them or not. (I would say so anyways, I have no idea about stocks and shares.)

I also think that this whole working-every-hour-of-the-day-to-prove-your-worth-at-a-job needs to stop. Your employer should see your commitment to the job from the hours you are there working. Not who doesn't have any place to be after so can stay until ten p.m. Come on now, huns. We shouldn't have to work nineteen hour days to get a promotion or be favoured in the workplace. How about working during the hours we are paid for should be the only deciding factor. I said what I said.

How to survive work? Win the lottery and quit, ha, ha. No, but seriously, turn off your notifications if you do have any work apps on your phone. Do not look at anything work related until you are in your working hours. Set yourself boundaries. Take those breaks, book time off and finish on time most days. Your mental health will thank you. Work smarter, huns, not harder.

Rubbish jobs

Glitter is my favourite colour, has been and will always be, but and I cannot stress this enough, it is not by any means a form of payment, currency or even a nice little bonus.

Many moons ago I had a job where I was actually paid in glitter. No, I wasn't Tinkerbell's PA. (That would be awesome by the way. Love ya, Tink, hun.) I was, shall we say, working as a form of makeup artist without the makeup or artist part and just adding glitter to people's faces for a fee at events. Oh no, no, no, not my fee. My fee was any colour glitter I wanted.

I was at uni during the glitter period and worked with/for someone in the field my degree was in. I had some amazing moments with said person but it was mainly for free or, ya know, glitter.

Now I am not one to look a gift horse in the mouth (kick a gift horse? No, no, don't be doing that), but I was a mature student with bills to pay and sadly my bank manager would not accept glitter. They weren't having any of it, not even in a delightful shade of hot pink. Petty Betty over here. Imagine turning up to the bank asking to deposit a pot of glitter.

Glitter aside, you can always tell when I hate a job I am at as I will always spend my lunch breaks or any free time between work tasks scrolling on my phone on social media trying to desperately be a part of another world. Any other world than this shitty one where I am demonstrating how to make nylon for a bunch of teens who wouldn't have noticed if I had set fire to my head and run off screaming.

I would always tell myself, *It's okay, Nik, a better job is coming. The job you love is coming.* Other than my current fulltime job (which I like, and not just saying that in case they read this and I get fired before I get a chance to become a bestselling author) alongside writing this absolute smash of a book, I have only ever loved one job. Which I was made redundant from as the world decided to have a pandemic and close everything. What a joy.

Pretty much everyone you speak to in the world will have had at least one job they hated. It's just the law in the world of work. However, I am a firm believer in not staying in a job you hate just because it is a job. Or just because it is a job that looks good to outsiders.

I am also a firm believer in not being told I should be grateful I even have a job. Yes, I know that, Carol, sheesh, but that doesn't mean I have to be all roses and kittens every day. It still and will always suck. God, Carol!

How to survive a rubbish job? Know better is coming and no matter what you do, never accept glitter as a form of payment.

Working from home

'You're on mute, hun. Hun, *you're on mute*! That little microphone icon, yes that's it. Tap that. There we go, hiya! Oh, I've lost you, your internet isn't great.'

Never a truer word spoken. I literally could just end this chapter there and we would all completely understand what I was talking about, no questions asked. Zoom are literally living their best lives. I have never uttered the word *mute* more times than I have in the last few years.

I find working from home an absolute dream. So if or when working from home becomes a drag, just remember this:

You can get up much later. I mean that commute from the kitchen to your home office is a joyous trip. This made it sound like I sleep in my kitchen. I can assure you I sleep in an actual bed, but you know what I mean.

You can control the temperature. Hot. Cold. Hot then cold. Cold then hot. The options are all yours. No more freezing your titties off with the office aircon because Susan will die if it gets turned off. Grow up, Susan!

You can wear what you want. The lounge suit has made a massive comeback and I for one am so happy for them. And you can always throw a fancy-shmancy top on for the Zoom call. Yes, I am not afraid to admit this.

Business on the top, party on the bottom, remember. Am I wearing a bra under my hoody? Who knows, huns. Even I have to check sometimes.

You can adjust the lighting accordingly. Urgh, how harsh are those office lights. Like, is it necessary to roast my eyeballs first thing of a morning. I now participate in a little desk lamp and feature lamp action. One I highly recommend.

Snacks and beverages on tap. Okay, this one could be a con too. Especially when you're trying to eat healthy. Before you know it, your desk is covered in M&Ms, Wotsits and half a bottle of gin (just kidding about the gin, boss, if you're reading this). Also on the food and beverage chatter, you can whack something in the oven for your lunch. All you gotta do is nip downstairs, chuck in a chicken breast and boom, you got yourself a hot lunch.

Your lunch break and evenings are more productive. My first working from home job included an hour lunch. What an absolute delight that was, the lunch break, I mean, the actual job sucked. Oh, what I would do with that time, I wouldn't even have enough time to tell you. I could go for a walk to the local park, sunbathe in the garden, pop into town. I mainly just went and sat downstairs and stared at my phone, but if I wanted to venture out I had time on my side, baby. So much time.

Plus, at the end of the day you are already home so can pop anywhere you like when things are still open. I mean I still just went downstairs and stared at my phone again, but if I wanted to I could have travelled absolutely anywhere. As long as I was back by nine a.m. the next day ready to tappity tap once more.

The only downside I find working from home is that you tend to do more work as there are no work friends to talk to. Although I would trade that for loungewear and a home cooked chicken breast lunch any day.

How to survive working from home? Get a grip and enjoy the freedom. By freedom I mean on your lunch and after work, obviously. I am tied to my desk for the rest of the day, duh!

Not being a morning person

Other than being told your plane is delayed or a Kate Spade item is out of stock, the sound of your alarm is the worst sound in the world. Like why? I have to be woken up from my beautiful slumber as it is, why does it have to be to the sound of a screeching arsehole. (My nickname for my alarm clock.)

I am old school when it comes to an alarm and I do not like to use my phone. So we could argue that I could use my phone and have some nice twinkling bells waking me up, but we all know I will do as I please and continue to moan about it, LOL.

The only time I am ever okay with being awake before ten a.m. is when I am going on holiday, and even then my alarm will go off and I will contemplate if I really want to go on this holiday or should I cancel. Fear not, huns, I am just a dramatic bitch and will, of course, never cancel my holiday in return for staying in bed.

I will, however, lie in bed every morning my alarm goes off and contemplate if I actually need my fulltime job (answer is always yes). Should I quit (answer it always no). Have I won the lottery yet (answer is once again always no, so damn childish).

I truly envy those people who can just jump out of bed without sobbing like a little brat every morning. Those people are true heroes or nutters, you choose. I am not one of those that snooze my alarm a billion times, but I am a grumpy son of a bitch every morning and will rip your face off if you speak to me. Thank god I work from home huh? Would be in jail otherwise.

I did try blasting a good song every morning as soon as I woke up. That lasted for about a week before I forgot and went back to the miserable bitch that I am. It did work for that week though. Oh, what a joy it was and I was such a delight.

The worst thing about not being a morning person is living with someone who is a morning person. They think if they are up everyone should be up when quite frankly, I think they should go outside and shut the fuck up. Don't you be wandering anywhere near me being a noisy wench. You take that shit elsewhere. I don't want to see or hear from you for another six hours. Sod off.

How to survive not being a morning person? You do you, hun. Tell the morning people to get fucked and enjoy being a grouch, hun. It's great!

Customers/clients

A work environment would be so much better without the customers and clients, right? I mean I know there would be no work environment and we would all be out of jobs. But my gosh, what a blissful place it would be, just getting on with your work, minding your own business without having to speak to any customers who are trying to make your day the absolute worst. Go away, hun. Not today. Not ever.

Most customers you encounter throughout your day are an absolute delight. Then you get those handful who try to kill you with their words. Won't listen to your advice, think they know everything and won't let you get a word in. Yep, don't worry, hun, I have plenty of time to stand here listening to you waffle on about why it's my fault they no longer stock your fave shampoo. Or, why it's my fault that you don't listen so you don't know what is happening and you just keep getting it wrong. Good grief.

The worst part about all of this as you literally cannot say a damn word. Just have to sit/stand there smiling like the Cheshire cat. *Nope, I'm not angry at all please go on boring me with your pointless story and shouting at me over something I have and will never have anything to do with. Please go ahead, it fills me with so much joy.*

I used to work at a store that sold cosmetics and a customer walked in asking for a mascara that was advertised when she was watching *Corrie* on Friday night. Cue my blank stare whilst I search for words that don't sound like me telling her to F off. *I don't know, hun. I wasn't in your house and nor did I watch* Corrie *last night. Even if I did I am pretty sure I would not have made a note of all the adverts to report back in case you came in with a query on one of them.*

Me: 'Oh, I am not sure, sorry, but we did have this new one in last week.'

Customer: 'Yes you do, it was on the first ad break on Friday night's *Corrie*. Seven-thirty p.m. it started. Had a woman in the advert.'

Me:

Customer: 'Oh this is ridiculous. You should know exactly what I am talking about.'

What!

Now I am no customer service expert but I am pretty sure I am not meant to ever know this information. Unless I was on the lookout for a mascara, watching *Corrie* on Friday night and did not fast forward through all the damn adverts. Even then I am pretty sure I would have forgotten by now.

Please step aside and let me go about my day and prepare for the next ridiculous questions that are due to come my way.

Surely there comes a time in everyone's lives where they understand that some things are really out of people's control. And surely there comes a time when they understand we are just doing our jobs so we can get paid to drink on the weekend and black out anything that ever took place here. Surely!

I truly believe everyone should work at least one shift in customer service. Mainly retail as we all know the amount of shit that goes down there. I am triggered just thinking about it.

From my experience you can pretty much tell the customers who have never worked in this industry in their lives. They are usually jerks with no care in the world for anyone else than themselves and what shit they are buying. No one cares about your new spatula, hun.

I am a firm believer that no one deserves to be treated like shit. It is super hard when you have to slap a smile on your face and pretend you aren't bothered by what Susan is moaning to you about. Which, as we all know, is completely beyond your control and waaaay above your pay grade. Yet here we are listening to Suzie (can I call you Suzie?) banging on about how she couldn't find a parking space and this has now led her to mention she will never shop here again.

Hey, Suzie hun, do I actually look like I give a tiny rat's arse? Because I promise you, babes, I do not. You and your shitty spatula can fuck off. (I never actually worked anywhere that sold spatulas but you catch my drift.)

How to survive customers? Get yourself a job that does not involve speaking to the general public on a daily basis. It is the only way to survive.

Bad customer service

People who work in customer service have a lot of crap thrown at them, but sometimes the roles can be reversed, and the worker becomes the absolute dick and you want to shove Suzie's spatula up their arses. Sorry, Suzie, hun.

I am sure I am not alone in the number of times I have received shitty customer service. It truly makes my blood boil, especially seeing the other side. Yes, we all have problems, but sadly in this job no one gives a damn. You must leave them at the door and smile as I kindly order a side of bacon to go with my pancakes.

Being someone who suffers with anxiety, bad customer service can really get to me and sometimes I can't help but take it personally. I often think if certain shitty customer service issues happened to someone who was really on the edge, this could turn into a life or death situation.

I was once in a well-known coffee shop. I had a lovely day out shopping and it was the first time I had ventured out in a while. I was so excited, had the best day and was now rewarding myself with a hot chocolate as a well done for making it through the day, and you know, because I desperately needed one. The server was soooo rude. He had got my order wrong and this was somehow my fault apparently. I kindly and politely mentioned that this was not what I ordered. He then slammed the correct drink down on the counter, practically throwing it at me in the process.

I was so upset and truly wanted to cry. To many this would have seemed like nothing and you would have left thinking, *Ooooo, what's rattled his cage*. But for me, given my circumstances that day, it left me feeling really rubbish and put a dampener on a great day.

It takes me back to the saying 'In a world where you can be anything be kind'.

No one knows what anyone is going through, and yeah, okay, the same could be said for the guy. He could have been going through some shit, but given his role you can't let it show. Also, you can't ruin someone's day just because yours has gone tits up. It is not cool, hun, not cool.

I purchased a car from a very big company that has adverts all over the place, and my gosh they are well trained with their customer service. By well-trained I mean they have an answer for everything and you will under no circumstances be having any form of compensation. Despite your car needing a whole new engine a month after purchasing it. Then having a courtesy car break down on you on the M4. The horror. I told them I could have died. They said, "Well you didn't, did you." Well no, do you really think I am making this call from beyond the grave? If I had died my first heaven phone call would not be to you, I can tell ya. Absolute bastards.

How to survive bad customer service? Brush it off and go about your day. If it is extremely bad, speak to a manager or higher up like I did with the coffee shop guy. Free hot chocolate? Don't mind if I do, thanks, hun. How to survive not giving bad customer service? Just don't be a dick. Simples.

Explaining yourself

Elton John once sang a song about sorry being a difficult word to say. You all know the one I mean without getting arrested for copyright laws. . I agree Elton, hun, unless you have anxiety then you just spit that word out like an alpaca.

You apologise for anything and everything and find yourself trying to explain yourself out of a situation that you aren't really in, in the first place.

Work colleague: 'Oh, xyz has gone wrong.'

Me: 'Oh my gosh, no. Well, I know I did xyz and then I made sure this was done and spoke to Sally, so it was all good to go.' Fuck sakes, Sally, why are you like this?.

I find myself digging and digging a huge hole that I am falling into when no one is saying it is my fault, it isn't even my fault, but now it looks like my fault because I sound guilty as shit. What even is this! I find myself so often explaining my version of events in the workplace as I feel if I don't, they are basically saying I can't do my job. I am scrambling to get myself out of a hole that I put my damn self in for absolutely no reason

I recently spoke to an amazing friend about this and she goes, 'Babe, you gotta stop. Just say oh no, way how can I help and carry on.'

Hannah, you are an absolute babe and could not be more right. I constantly feel like people are on the attack and then whoosh, my guard goes up, the guns come out (not literally, obviously) and I am trying to fight a fight that's not even mine. A fight that doesn't really exist.

We find ourselves explaining things so much that none of it even makes sense any more. Most of the time we don't owe anyone an explanation. If they think we did something, let them think that. If they were worthy of being in your life they would have your back and know it wasn't you.

This goes for all life situations you find yourself in. With friends, family, partners, the workplace. Obviously if they are about to fire you for something you haven't done then you need to speak out. But if it is just an issue that has nothing to do with you, just keep it quiet.

How to survive explaining yourself? In a word, don't. And I genuinely mean it for this one. A lot of us spend our lives trying to explain ourselves in a situation, when in reality these idiots don't deserve it. If you start to feel like you have to explain yourself, remove yourself from that situation asap.

Public transport

Public transport is a huge no from me. I'm not here for the waiting around and then the walking from said transport to my destination. I'm more of a roll out of the vehicle and into the building in front of me kinda girl. You know, lazy!

This also leads me into another thing I don't like. Strangers. Or just people in general. 'Is this seat taken?' Yes, it is, now off you fuck, hun!

I used public transport a lot in uni and good grief, it still gives me flashbacks. Waiting in the rain as the delayed announcement flashes up. My hair blowing like it's trying to escape to somewhere a bit less shit (you and me both, babes).

Being shoved in a carriage like a cow on their way to the slaughterhouse (sorry, vegans) is just the worst, especially first thing in the morning. Don't get me wrong, I don't want to be herded like a cow anytime of the day but in the morning that is just uncalled for and downright rude. And just for an added bonus, you'll always get that one person who is an absolute bellend, has no awareness of person space and finds it acceptable to have their junk in your face at seven on a Monday morning. Not today, Satan.

A train to London does not count. Not a huge fan but it's better than a certain type of bus that shall remain nameless. I can see why they only used to charge a pound. It was like an episode of *The Flintstones* on that shit.

Please, huns, do not get taking a train to London confused with using the Tube whilst in London. (London traffic is next level plus where does one even park in the big smoke? Does Charlie make a couple of quid on the side for parking at the palace, by any chance?) 'Let's get the Tube, it will be much cheaper.' Babes, I don't care if I have to sell a kidney to pay for the taxi, you can tube it on your own, hun. Enjoy!

I've taken the Tube. (Do we say taken the Tube? Used the Tube? Slid on the Tube? Oooer!) Anyways, I've participated in a little light London Tube action in my time. And on one occasion I almost died.

Now, this is not me being dramatic. There I was, minding my own business, waiting for the train to arrive and a warning message flashed on the screen to evacuate. I glanced around and everyone was just standing there, other than one guy who grabbed his girlfriend's arm and dragged her out. Could have been a coincidence. Could have been an attack. I wasn't hanging around to find out.

In horror I ran to the lifts. Then I remembered the first rule in an emergency of this kind: don't take the lifts. Damn it! Now remember my lazy ass and how it feels about walking, now I've got to find some stairs and make the climb like I'm in an episode of *SAS*.

I find the stairs and there's a warning on them. *Only use in an emergency as it is the equivalent of climbing over 140 flights of stairs*. Right! Do I want to chance it down here and hope for the best or take the stairs and hope my knees don't give in on the way up?

Stairs it is. And not just any stairs, oh no no. Those winding stairs that are much smaller on one side. Requiring very careful footing. So now I have to be as fast as I can, watch I don't fall back down and act like it's no big deal, I climb stairs all the time, whilst trying to hide my breathing from sounding like I've just outrun Mo Farah at a marathon.

Pretty sure I saw a white light at one point, where I was pretty glad and hoping Jesus would come and take me. Not to be dramatic or anything but I almost died!

Moral of the story is… yeah, I got nothing.

I don't not use public transport because I think I'm fancy (well I am, but ya know) or because I can afford to always take taxis. I have absolutely no business handing over my cash for a twenty-minute taxi ride when the Tube would have taken a nanosecond. If I am lacking in funds and have zero pounds for a taxi I just won't go; even if I could use public transport, I'd rather miss out, ha, ha. Lame, I know. I just do not and will not like it. As Hearsay would say, *Pure and Simple*.

And even when it's my only option, I will do it with a face like a slapped arse and moan the entire journey. You are welcome, my friend. Oh, and there had better be snacks!

How to survive public transport? Order an Uber and be done with it. If you see me on public transport in the near future, please panic, as it must mean the world is ending and I'm trying to flee to safety. And I suggest you do the same. Sell a kidney, your sister, older brother, your cat.* Anything. Just do not get on that train/bus. You have been warned.

Please do not actually sell any organs, pets or siblings. Maybe sell a goldfish at a push or an ex-partner, as they probably had it coming, the ex, not the goldfish.

Peeing in public

I like to think of myself as a fully formed grownup. I mean, I pay my own bills, always make sure there is fuel in my car; I keep my niece and nephew fed and watered and most importantly alive in my care and I always keep myself hydrated. See, grownup! But you can guarantee on any car journey I am going to have to pee. I do the grownup thing and pee before I leave but it is like my bladder always knows when we arrive somewhere and it's like, 'Ooh, we are here. I'm excited. Let's get this going. Where's the toilets at?'

Finding a toilet in public is always sooooo difficult. Why are there not more of them? We all have to use them. Is this some sort of conspiracy?

When COVID hit, public toilets shut up shop. COVID knows when you need a pee and it is not playing.

Settle in, it is story time, huns...

It was a glorious summer's day. The sun was beaming down. Not a cloud in the sky. Birds sang. I smiled (that is a shocker it itself).

We stuffed the car to the brim, because of course you need a car full of crap to head to the beach for three hours. It is just standard practice. My sunnies and hat were perfectly in place. I looked like an extra from a bad version of *Riviera* but I was ready nonetheless.

If it wasn't for COVID life would have been pretty darn perfect. But here we are, COVID laws left right and centre and my bladder wanting to explode out of my body to check out the views and see what was going on.

Upon reaching said beach destination. I calmly glanced around, hoping my bladder couldn't see what I could see. Zero toilets. Nothing, nada Not even a shed that had someone been converted into a toilet was allowed to be occupied.

Now I am one of those annoying people who if I have to pee, I have to pee. And everyone else's day will be filled with my moaning if it does not happen. No, I cannot just quietly sit and cross my legs. I need the whole family beach party to hear my dilemma and to feel my pain. Not that they ever care. I just get a shut up Nik and they go on their merry way. Bit rude but whatever.

So, here we are, bladder full. Toilet shed shack closed. I am not one for peeing in a bush, I can't seem to get the angle right these days and end up just peeing all down my legs. Classy! So, I did what any other completely sane person would do is this predicament, I used my nephew's potty. All I can and will say on the matter is I am very thankful for tinted windows and masks so I could relieve myself incognito and in the privacy of the back seats of Carol's Nissan. Thanks, Carol, hun.

Sidenote, my lower body is in dire need of some gym action (and upper body, now we come to mention it) as the pain from squatting over the potty the next day was no joke. Literally felt like I had run a marathon. Again, not that I like to be dramatic or anything.

How to survive a life without public toilets? Grow a penis or invest in one of those she-wees, whichever one suits you best. I am all about choices here. Although, I do highly recommend a potty, especially if you hit the gym regularly. You will have no issues whatsoever squatting over that bad boy. I would definitely do it again. Well, I actually did a few weeks later at another beach. Tried, tested and you are very welcome. I have never wished I had a penis more, well, ever actually.

The beach

No, this isn't a section on how to survive a shark attack. Not a survival guide, remember? Although now we are here, just give it a punch in the nose or stick your finger in its eye and it should be on its merry way. Might take a chunk out of your leg in the process, but who am I to judge a shark's diet.

As we were, I am a firm believer in if you have a body (your own, not one to dispose of), whack a swimsuit on and take it to the beach. Boom you got yourself beach body ready.

Sidenote, this made it sound like I was condoning and planning a murder and the burial of said murdered body. The only killing we'll be doing is of our swimwear because we look sooooo damn good. (I know, I am hilarious.)

I am also a firm believer in being shit scared taking said body to the beach, (again I'm referring to my own living body). Disclaimer, any reference to a body and/or killing it throughout this book has a hundred percent nothing to do with anything that the police should be involved in. There has been a mistake, Officer. Noted? Good. On we go.

Beach days are the best, right? The sound of the waves crashing is like no other. That is exactly what my heaven would sound like, crashing waves, and it would smell of coconut. It is the perfect time to chill but for so many of us it can be super stressful. Especially with so many Judge Judy wannabes out there. Back off, hun, and let me live my best life here in peace. If my wobbly bits offend you that right there sounds like a you problem. Ta-ra, babes, ta-ra.

We always give ourselves a pep talk, yet we still continue to stand in the mirror pulling apart everything we don't like.

If we want to go to the beach we should just go to the beach without worrying about other people or how we will look. People are arseholes. Give them something to talk about.

How to survive a beach day? If you truly aren't feeling beach body ready, get yourself some swimwear or an outfit that you really, really, love. Even if you don't feel one hundred percent your best or look how you would like to look. Choose something you feel really comfortable in, put it on and enjoy the day. (Swearing warning) Fuck everyone else. I know it really is easier said than done but it is the truth, nonetheless. No one is a hundred percent happy and comfortable with the way they look, regardless of what they say.

Remember, savour every moment. Life is short. Plus, you never know when that sneaky shark is swimming around looking for a snacky snack, and you, my friend, are the perfect snack looking all gorge in your beachwear. Enjoy.

A bad hair day

Okay, cool got all my clothes out ready for work, jewellery has been chosen, straightened my hair to within an inch of its life. We are all good to go in the morning and with all this planning we get extra time in bed, woo.

What the fuck is that sound. Oooooh yeah, my alarm. Calm down, hun, I am getting up. Thank god I didn't have to get up any earlier to straighten my hair. Just run a brush through it after a shower and off we go.

Narrator: But we were not good to go. In fact, her hair looked better before she had even straightened it compared to what can now only be described as an abandoned bird's nest. Even the birds couldn't cope with the sight.

Good grief, hun. I'm not sure what I was doing whilst sleeping last night but it looks as if I have been living in a bush out in the garden for six weeks. Maybe, if I just brush this part down and spray it with a shit ton of hairspray — Elnett, we can make it work. Nope. Straighteners are going to have to come back out. Which means I wasted all my time last night doing it and now I will probably be late. What's that saying? Better late than ugly, right?

I will arrive late and still look like a sack of unwanted potatoes. It's just the way it is. Soz, huns. Look away!

Healthy eating

It's Monday. It's nine a.m., you've just had your breakfast. It was two sticks of carrots and a handful of grapes, if anyone was wondering. You look at the clock; it must be lunch time now surely. Nope still nine a.m. The hunger is real and you can almost, definitely, one hundred percent feel the anger creeping in.

You walk to the kitchen. Open the fridge. *Maybe there is a healthy snacky snack I can munch on.* The fridge is empty. You open it again as your trust issues go as far as your fridge. Still empty. You contemplate sucking on an ice cube just to bide the time. Thankfully there isn't any ice left either, as that would have ended with a blow torch and trip to A&E. You go back to the fridge. Something healthy and tasty must have appeared by now. Still nothing. You look at the clock. Still nine a.m.

You start to question if this is all worth it. Then you catch a glimpse of your double chin in the mirror and jump with fright thinking Chewbacca had just broken in. Ain't no snacks here, hun, keep it moving.

You spend the next few hours wallowing in self-pity, hoping to distract yourself from the deep, dark hunger inside. You take a look at the clock. Still nine a.m.

Why is it that you can do your hair exactly the same every day, sometimes you will look like you should definitely be on TV or at least IG famous. Other days you look like you should belong on TV too but more of the *Crimewatch* kinda shows ya know?

My hair is my pride and joy and if it even goes slightly out of place, I lose my mind. When you get all dolled up for a night out, your hair is perfect then five minutes before you leave it has all gone tits up and now you can't go out because the fringe that you haven't got has parted slightly. What is this life.

The worst is when you are out, steaming, living your best life, you go to the toilet towards to end of the night and you literally look like you haven't brushed your hair or washed your face in three weeks. But who cares, you are drunk and loving life.

How to survive a bad hair day? Go back to bed, cry and pray that tomorrow is different. Get drunk every time it goes tits up (jokes, jokes, don't do this). Or, now we are all grownups (apparently), petty but whatever, whack it up in a pony or if all else fails stick on a hat and work that headgear.

sitting watching a film with no snacks in your hands, like some kind of peasant. Nothing to dip your hand into and let your heart be filled with joy.

Don't even get me started on a trip to the cinema with no snacks. Let's just say I am grateful for the pandemic and I haven't had to go through such horror. What am I supposed to do without snacks? Just sit there like some kind of movie bore and just watch the film? I mean I know I have usually got through all my snacks before the trailers have even finished but come on. I'm not some kind of animal.

Now I'm no expert but time definitely stands still when you are eating healthy. I use the term eating healthy as a diet just sends me over the edge with panic. Plus, trying to refrain from eating six waffles, twelve pancakes, eight packets of ready salted crisps and a small village isn't really a diet now, is it. Eating a carrot stick and a boiled egg is what normal people eat. My eggs just happen to be covered in chocolate. And my carrot sticks are bread sticks dipped in some sort of garlic butter. Aaaah, bliss.

How to survive 'healthy eating'? Just as you're about to eat a family size bar of chocolate, right as it is millimetres away from your lips, hire someone to throw a couple of carrots or a stick of celery in there instead. You can thank me later.

That should full on without a doubt be a real job.

'WANTED. Person to knock junk food out of my hands and throw healthy snacks into my pie hole.' Salary would be like 20k minimum. Why is it whenever you are on track to get back on the vegetable bandwagon, there is always some occasion to attend? Like a birthday meal, coffee and cake with the bestie, or just your Saturday night snacky snacks. Life is always sent to test us, huns. Watch your back or it will have you balls deep in a McDonald's Big Mac and large fries, two happy meals and a couple of McFlurrys. Good grief!

You look at the clock again. Still nine a.m. What kind of sorcery is this?

The days come and they are super hard, then the nights come and they are even harder. The evenings just

Gaining weight — absolute cheek

There I was choosing some rings to wear to work (thought I'd better make an effort), only one fitted. Why, you ask? Because I am a fat bastard, that's why. My fingers seem to have become a family pack of pork sausages (or meat free if you're vegan), and probably not even the good ones. Those sad, boring ones at the back of the freezer that you save for a last minute meal emergency that you hope you will never have.

Sausage fingers aside, I stayed positive and even made up a song about how much of a fat bastard I am. 'Twas a joyous occasion. We all had a laugh. By all, I mean me and my eight sausage pals and an extra helping of thumbs. (As in they are big too, not that I have extra thumbs. Good grief.)

Screaming on the inside, but smiling on the outside as fear not, huns, I am in the process of doing something about it. She says for the millionth time.

It's my fault that my fingers now represent the Teletubbies and their pals, I am fully aware of this fact. Will I still bitch and moan about it? Of course I will, duh. I mean if I will eat a gigantic packet of crisps and a sharing bag of jelly tots of a weekend, what did I expect?

It is always such a shock though, isn't it. Like you've just seen a ghost or an ex. (I would much rather be possessed than see any of my exes, and I am sure the feeling is mutual.) When you catch yourself in the mirror wearing that top that fitted last year, you jump with disbelief. *Who is that horrifying image staring back at me and why is she wearing my top? Oh good god, it's bloody me, isn't it.* 'What the hell happened?' I whisper to myself as I pile a pack of giant buttons in my mouth. *I went for a walk yesterday. How dare my body defy me like this.*

I must now drown my sorrows and cheer myself up with a little snacky snack to snack nibble on. Maybe go out for a meal? I mean, that might work. Some steak and sweet potatoes will definitely put a smile on my double chins. Until the next day when I try to find something to wear again and me and my family pack of sausages are completely screwed.

When clothing in your wardrobe doesn't fit, you feel a sense of betrayal. Like, why couldn't you have just lied to me and worked your magic to make it fit. 'Why you acting like this?' I say to my T-shirt that is now clinging to my hips for dear life. 'Do you want to have a nice day out with me because you are going the wrong way about it.'

How to survive gaining weight? Have your mouth stitched up. I joke, I joke... Kinda. We can't change the past so focus on the now and the future and do something to change it. Unless you are healthy and happy with the way you are, then you go, girl!

Clothes shopping

There I was, standing in front of the mirror, smiling at how fabulous my hair and makeup looked that day. It would have been a great day, had I not just walked into a high street store and picked up three dresses and a skirt. That was my first mistake. My second was that I thought these would actually fit, so I casually and excitedly walked towards to fitting room.

That's when everything took a turn. Had it not been for the fact I had no business spending this money on dresses today, I would have found myself in a heap on the floor.

But 'No!', I cried out, putting the shits up several other women in said fitting room. '*No*! We will not let these items make us feel shit about ourself, Nik. Yes, we have put on a bit of timber, who hasn't?' (If you haven't, please don't tell me. Good for you but please fuck off out of my face. Much love, hun).

I am not living in denial, the sizing sucked. And I stood there looking like a sack of potatoes that definitely needed to be thrown out two days ago.

If you have had the pleasure of reading my other books, just kidding there are no other books *yet,* but I have always wanted to say that. If you have read anything I have written before you may have come across an article I wrote for a magazine. What is this article, I hear you cry. Well, huns, I wrote about how shitty sizes are in stores and how it impacts our mental health. I wrote that article a good few years ago and the situation is nowhere near getting better.

In fact, it is worse. I have even found lately that it isn't just adults clothing that they are screwing with. Kids' clothes are ridiculously different sizes and it is not great. I'm sorry, what? Yes, not only shall we make women feel shit about themselves but let's make kids' sizes all over the place too. Best start their body issues young.

I always find when you are looking for something in particular you can never find anything. Then when you are poor and just go in for a browse the stores are full of wonderous items just begging for you to buy them. Don't start with me, babes, I ain't falling for it.

It's like the stores know when you are in a rush for a last minute outfit and hide all the good stuff from you. Absolute cheek. Yes, it may be my fault that it's last minute; it may also be that I have only now decided to go out or I have only just been paid. Not so silly now, is it.

When you have a bucket full of cash to spend and a whole wardrobe to buy and nothing fits or makes you look like JLo it is a real kick in the shitter.

How to survive clothes shopping? Grab your bucket of cash and have a lovely time. If your bucket is looking a little empty (same, babes, same) just have a look about for inspo, for when you can buy something. Don't let the stupid sizing get you down. It's not you, it is them! LOL, imagine turning up to a shopping centre with an actual bucket of money. I love how I make myself laugh. Oh, what a joy I am.

Loving/not loving yourself

After all this chat of sausage fingers and sacks of potatoes, I thought we'd best flip the script before people start thinking this is a cookbook. A very rubbish cookbook, might I add.

We are always told to love ourselves no matter what we look like and there is so much truth in this *but* it really is difficult to do sometimes. We are all different shapes and sizes and what is amazing to someone else is not to others. What I believe stops us loving ourselves is the outside chatter and how we are told in magazines, TV shows, people in the street, if you aren't slim, you aren't beautiful.

This is a complete and utter lie and these idiots who say or write this shit need to have a word with themselves and fuck off. It can be so damaging. Yes, we all need to be healthy but we can still be beautiful with a few extra pounds, and the number on the scale or on your clothing does not determine how gorgeous you are. And that works both ways, a larger or smaller number does not matter. It does not define you.

The way we live our lives is often due to how society tells us we should. We are made to believe that bigger is ugly and we should want to change ourselves if we are over the size they say is 'right'. I say take your size and fuck off, hun.

When it comes to dressing a curvier body so many people have the attitude that if you're bigger you couldn't possibly look nice. Absolute shit, hun. Your size does not mean your outfits suck. I, in fact, know how to dress and can look way more amazing in what I've put together than a lot of other girls, slim or curvy. So put that theory in your pipe and smoke it.

It is truly hard to love your body when you are constantly being told that you are not right. Nope, that colour hair isn't the one. Those freckles should be covered up. No wait, they are on trend again, show them proudly. Please do not wear that top, you look terrible, you are too big. Oh, don't wear that top, you are too small. What do these people want from us and who even are these people?

I was on a work's night out recently (I know who would have thought it) and they are all such beautiful women with beautiful bodies and it made me feel utterly shit. Nothing to do with those amazing ladies, they are beautiful inside and out; it is me, my brain and my body issues.

For the next few days after the night out I didn't feel myself. I was super glad that I went and enjoyed the company. Yet I left feeling deflated and I couldn't put my finger on it until halfway through the following week. The last time I went out I had lost some weight. Now I was left feeling like a heffalump and not the cute kind.

My mind has been making me feel so rubbish that I am just not myself. Yes, I could just get my butt on the treadmill but it takes time. I wish you could just click your fingers and look how you want.

Most of us have issues with our bodies, even those that have a fabulous body to someone else. There are always areas we don't like about ourselves and that's fine. What is not fine is to let it consume your thoughts like I have done. I try to be grateful for what I do have. Thankful that my legs get me from A to B. Thankful for my arms so I can do my hair or even write this book. I know it is hard, huns, but we have to keep trying to love ourselves. Download an affirmations app, look in the mirror every day and say one thing you love about yourself. Some homework for you, huns.

We are also condemned if we do actually love ourselves. Like umm, excuse me, hun but we think you need to be knocked down a peg or two. You shouldn't possibly be this happy with yourself. You must be so full of yourself. Literally cannot win!

How to survive loving/not loving yourself? We may not love our bodies all of the time but try and focus on the parts you do love. Your hair, your legs, the way your eyes light up when you smile. Love each part individually and gradually you will love everything about you. It doesn't mean you don't want to change anything; it just means you love yourself the way it is now and if you're anything like me, you are open for improvement.

A bad mental health day/period

A bad mental health day can creep up on you like a parking ticket. You feel it is probably coming but you live in hope that it doesn't. No, sir, it wasn't me parking illegally for three hours. No way, I am a law-abiding citizen.

I wish I could tell my brain no. I mean, sometimes you can, but quite rudely it doesn't always listen. Like, excuse me, you're my brain, how dare you defy me.

You can be having an amazing few days. Everything is all fine, la, la, la, having a great day, then boom!

Brain: 'We should be suspicious and very sad about something.'

Me: 'Oh really, what? But everything is great. I'm having a lovely day.'

Brain: 'Yeah, but we shouldn't be happy. We shouldn't be enjoying this.'

Me: 'Oh yeah, you're right. We should probably go home.'

In December 2021 I went on an amazing trip to New York. (I say the date like it was fifteen years ago, ha.) It was postponed from the year before due to obvious reasons that we will not discuss. I was sooo excited. It was all I spoke about for months. I spent hours booking things, putting itineraries together, watching YouTube videos and looking back at my photos from four years ago when we went for my thirtieth birthday.

The two weeks leading up to it were horrendous. All the travel info kept changing and as much as I tried to stay positive, I really thought that it may not happen. I know this sounds like first world problems and I sound like a whiney bitch, but things like this really keep me going and having something to look forward to really helps how my brain works.

We finally made it to the hotel in London the night before our flight. Our tests had come back negative and we were ready to go. Except my brain was not. I felt numb and I wanted to cry. I didn't know why and that made me feel even worse. Here I was, a few hours away from visiting my favourite place in the world, and I wasn't excited.

Even once we had landed and were driving in a taxi to our hotel in Manhattan, I was trying to force myself to be excited.

The last time we went I was bouncing off the walls. I couldn't contain my excitement and I was like a child for the whole trip. Why wasn't I feeling the same, or even more excited, as it had been a long time coming. Why did I just want to curl up into a ball and sleep.

Thankfully, I've started to realise in the last year or so, it is my brain making me think these things and not me. I try to fight it off and give myself a pep talk and my brain a telling off. How dare it ruin this incredible trip for me. A trip that I couldn't stop thinking about every day for the last two years.

I wake up now and again with an overwhelming feeling of anxiety and I hate it. Absolutely nothing had changed from the few hours before, when I went to sleep. I hadn't read anything, spoken to anyone, or thought anything that would make me stress out. Yet here I was in a ball of chaos trying to talk myself off the ledge, so to speak, so I could start my day.

Someone said online recently that when they start to feel their anxiety creeping in, they tell it out loudly to fuck off. Genius idea and one I have started to do. I know everyone has different levels of anxiety and it may not work for you, but it is worth a go. Even if it makes your anxiety levels a little lower, that can only be a good thing, right?

I have suffered with anxiety for a few years now and think I always had a tiny bit of it most of my life. It was only when my dad passed away in 2015 that it became pretty bad. Then, flash forward a few years and a global pandemic, and I am left a complete mess.

2020 really fucked with my head as it did for many people and I found my life with nothing much in it. We couldn't see friends, we couldn't go anywhere. To think that at one point we were limited to an hour walk a day just blows my mind and the reason now why I still don't like to go out that much.

It took me a good while to venture out shopping again and shopping is my all-time favourite thing to do in a life. I just adore it and I hate that the feeling of excitement was taken away from me. It's now met with fear and anger and I would rather stay home than have to deal with all these emotions.

I still struggle with going anywhere if I am not with my family. I need someone there who understands, and someone who knows what is going through my mind and that I am struggling with just one look.

I have recently been asked out for work drinks. I said yes and I planned my outfit to go. Then the night was cancelled and I was pretty relieved. Then someone decides to rearrange it. Oh no. I am not really in the head space any more. The moment has passed and I don't want to go. You go on ahead, guys, it's a no from me, hun. If you say no you look boring, miserable and like you don't want to bond with the team. Which is completely untrue in this scenario as I actually really like everyone I work with. Will they understand if I say no? Will they understand if I go then have to bail out after an hour or so?

As much as I don't want my anxiety holding me back in life, I am not in the best head space to be in a situation I really don't want to be in. I won't sit there with fake smiles and this was long before my anxiety keeps trying to kill me. If I'm going it's because I really want to and am looking forward to it. Wish me luck, huns. I know you are just dying to hear all about my boring, non-existent, personal life.

Whenever I find myself in a downward spiral, after lying on the floor crying for several minutes, I try to focus on the small things that I can control and that brings me joy.

Lately I light my Christmas candle from Bath and Body Works that I bought in New York. It instantly makes me smile and makes me think of the amazing time I had in

New York. When I'm feeling low, I will light it no matter what time of the year.

Not as often as I light my candle (as I am always 'trying' to eat healthily, so childish), I'll make myself a hot chocolate. I have the Costa powder and it is the best hot chocolate you can make yourself, and of course, I add one extra teaspoon more than the packaging suggests, sue me. It makes me smile with every sip and I just feel comforted and warm and fuzzy inside.

I'm not saying lighting a candle and having a hot chocolate will cure your mental health problems. Although, that would actually be great. Focusing on things that bring you joy will bring you back out of the darkness little by little. I actually reached out to someone on a down day recently to tell them I was sad and feeling super low. I haven't known her long but I knew she would understand. The short chat made me feel better, and even though I know I'm not alone, it is still nice to hear it now and again. She made me smile through the tears and I am truly grateful for her. Some days no matter what you do, it does not make you feel better and that is fine too. Sometimes you have to just be and let it pass. Always know that it will get better even when it feels like there is no way out.

People are often shocked when they find out I suffer with my mental health; fake it till you make it, right? Which is why I think I struggle believing people will understand.

I also make sure I have things around me that make me happy. For me it's literally anything and everything I have bought in New York. I've even changed the background on my work laptop to a photo I took in New York, so I start and end the day with a smile.

I understand everyone's mental health struggles are different and some days no number of candles or hot chocolate will help make me smile. But just try it sometimes as it could be that comfort you need to make you feel you again.

Whatever is going on in the world please always remember that your feelings are valid. No matter how small or big you may think they are, always speak to someone. Keeping things to yourself really does make it seem so much bigger. Trying to carry a heavy box on your own can be impossible but having another person to help will ease the strain. Trust me.

How to survive a bad mental health day/period? Really try and tell yourself that it will pass. You don't really feel these things, it's your brain telling you that you should. Try and fight it; be louder than your brain and tell it to shut the fuck up. Always remember you are never alone and there are millions of others feeling exactly the same. Reach out to someone, it really does help. Sometimes we need that little extra help and need to speak to a professional. This is okay too. Getting the help you need is brave. Making that doctors appointment is a huge, scary step but a very brave one that could save your life.

Social media

Social media is a great invention. (Don't tell Zuckerberg I said that.) It is a great way to keep in touch with people, a great place for inspiration and perfect for seeing how your fave celebrity is doing. I always love to see what Katherine Ryan had for lunch or how H from Steps is spending his bank holiday.

It is a great outlet and one that is for sure a blessing and a curse. All rolled into a pretty box with a gorgeous bow, dipped in chocolate and delivered with a Range Rover. Reality, it's a recycled box from three Christmases ago, the bow is from your dog's last trip to the hair salon, the chocolate is out of date and the Range Rover is totally yours but only for the next thirty minutes on this test drive.

We spend hours and hours a week scrolling through social media. I just love it every Monday when my phone tells me my screen time is up by 110%, a hundred and nine of it spent on the socials. Cheers, hun.

I always try to use social media for inspiration and enjoy the pretty pictures and laugh at the funny reels. I don't begrudge anyone having more than me or something I want. I find this aspirational and something to keep me focused on my goals and work towards. I don't mind it at all, unless it isn't real.

We are all guilty of only posting our highs in life and when we look our best. Why wouldn't we? Who wants to see a post of me on a Sunday afternoon, in my Winnie the Pooh PJs, no makeup, hair three or four days old, no bra and my eyes all puffy from crying at yet another film where the dog doesn't make it. But why? Stop making these films!

Only posting your best moments is completely fine, but you need to remember when you look at that perfect family photo that this probably took about an hour to take. Maybe some bribery and possibly the only time they spent together that week. We must remember that others are only posting their best moments too.

I personally find reality stars are the worst for this. They are catapulted to fame super-fast, most didn't really work for it and now they are reaping all the rewards. It seems to get to their heads and they forget that a few weeks ago they were their audience too. Watching a famous person on Instagram posting their trip to Chanel and them desperately wanting that life too.

They forget that they are just normal people who just happened to be on a TV show for a few weeks. They now have this platform to change their lives and do amazing things whilst doing it. But instead a lot of them choose to be fake. Posting all their free shit and making out they have earned this lifestyle.

There seems to be a trend over the last couple of years, where people post the 'Instagram versus reality' yet sadly even their reality is mostly staged. Even their 'ugly' photo is staged, because no one wants to actually look their most shitty self and share it with the world.

I am all for the body positive posts that seem to be taking over the social media world lately but again, sooo freaking staged. Their message is great, their execution is all wrong. Posting photos of the rolls on your stomach when you sit down or showing your stretch marks on a few posts and telling people to love their bodies is great. But so many are just doing it for likes and followers.

I followed a beauty influencer once, who then became a fashion influencer and then quickly turned into a 'body positive' influencer. She saw that they were getting more likes and followers than the beauty ones were. As I watched from the sidelines you could see just how unauthentic this was, yet people were still buying in to her.

Social media is a place of smoke and mirrors where people often post to make themselves look better and for others to lust over what they have. A lot of people love to make themselves feel superior and for us to all feel crap that we don't have what they do.

So many post fabulous family days, full of baking cupcakes, smiling and laughter. 'The perfect day with my perfect family.' That is amazing and I am so happy for you but we all know this is bullshit. We all know baking those cakes involved shouting, stress and telling the kids to get their damn hands out of the raw eggs.

Someone who is struggling to have kids or has a child with a disability or illness who can't do those things is looking at your posts and feeling really shit about themselves. We forget it isn't real and it's just a pretty photo for social media so everyone can see how wonderful they are.

It's the same when people post transformation photos. We as an audience only see the final outcome and think urgh, why can't I look like that. What we don't see and forget to think of is all those months/years of hard work. All the blood, sweat and tears. Yes, they may post a little video of themselves in the gym, but what they don't post is them lying in bed each morning giving themselves a pep talk to get to that gym. Or talking themselves out of having yet another cheat meal.

With these kinds of posts, it isn't really the person posting's fault how you react to it. It is up to us to remember it is all smoke and mirrors, baby. Your family is great too. Your body is great and gets you from A to B and you can change it too, if you wish.

I try to be more mindful when I post these days. If I am posting a fun family day out with my niece and nephew I try to write something in the caption to show it wasn't all perfect. I am guilty of posting my new purchases and not thinking about how someone is sitting looking at it who may not be able to pay their mortgage this month. I honestly do not post for people to feel bad about themselves. I don't have kids. I don't have my own house.

It isn't like I am trying to make my life out to be perfect. Posting my handbags is my version of posting a family photo.

That New York holiday I posted? I saved for over a year for that. The upgrade to first class? It only cost me a few hundred pounds. (I did actually clarify this when I posted about the upgrade.) My new Kate Spade handbag? I saved for that and made sure when I walked into that store I knew actually what I could and couldn't afford.

I find myself sharing these kinds of posts rather than boring daily life as that is what social media has trained us in to thinking that is what we should be posting.

No one wants to see me nine a.m. on a Monday, in my hoody and joggers, crying at my desk because the weekend is over and I didn't get enough sleep last night. (I don't actually cry but I whinge and moan like a little bitch.) But no, I don't post that. I post myself tappity tapping at my fancy laptop, my nails all fresh and a smile on my face.

How to survive social media? Always remember no one is posting their bad days. People post for likes and followers and that picture perfect post where everyone is smiling and having the best time isn't even real. It might be for that split second, but everyone has problems and shit days they aren't posting. On the other side, these days it is so important to be mindful about what you're posting. I don't mean over thinking every post. Just be aware of how certain things make people feel.

Being a control freak

My anxiety has turned me into a, okay, a huge control freak. It needs it to be my way or I'm not doing it. And that's not because I'm like wwwah, I want my own way; it's because I know what I like and I'm comfortable with what I like. So soz but if you're not giving me full details I'm not coming. To be honest, these days even if you gave me a play-by-play, minute-by-minute agenda, I still probably won't be coming LOL. Soz, huns, I suck I know.

I remember a time when I was at school and we were planning a lovely day trip to the beach. We were in sixth form, a few of us could drive, it was going to be great. The day came and all the plans and details were up in the air. A friend was arranging the times and says, 'Cool, I'll go and pick Nikki up."

My bestie was like, 'Nooooo, the hell you will. You have to call her first otherwise you will get there and she just won't come as she will feel on the spot.'

My girl had my back. She was one hundred million percent right. Thank the lord for her or I would have missed out on a lush day. Thanks, Nat, babes. I bet she can't even remember it, yet to me it meant so much that she understood who I was and what I needed from the situation. Friend goals right there.

I'm the type of person who needs to know exactly where we are going, who is going and how long we roughly plan on being there. If it goes into the night I want to be wearing an appropriate outfit. Do I need beverages and snacks? Like, there is just so much to consider. What kind of psychopath do you think I am, just grabbing my phone and heading out the door on a whim. Ah, I really wish I could do this. What bliss that would be.

My car broke down on a trip to my sister's house recently and we had to walk home. It is around a 20/25 minute walk but I was so not prepared for this. I had flip flops on, not trainers. I didn't have a drink. I had left my sunglasses at home. What kind of crazy bastard thinks this is acceptable for me?

I am thankfully fully aware of how crazy I sound but I need what I need or do I? I actually did walk home that day, in my flip flops with no sunglasses. Thankfully my sister provided the hydration otherwise I would have had to call the coast guard and air ambulance to come get me. Okay so maybe I don't need these things I just want them to be comfortable. But hey it's my life why shouldn't I feel comfortable in it?

I love to be the planner of all outings these days. Booking holidays, arranging a night out, a shopping trip, whatever. It doesn't mean I am going to book everything to my liking, I always plan with everyone in mind as I know how it feels. It just means I can feel comfortable and excited about going. If I'm not, well then, you're on your own, babes.

Unless it was a huge life event like a birthday party or a wedding etcetera, if I don't like or vibe with someone who is going, you won't be seeing me there. I have spent far too many nights out smiling through gritted teeth when someone horrible is there. Removing myself from the situation is what is best for my mental health.

How to survive being a control freak? I cannot and will not, ha, ha. Call me a whiney brat but sometimes you just gotta do what's best for you.

Not just living for the weekend

It's Friday, I'm in love, wooooo this is fun. Saturday is going to be great, and then we blink and Sunday night comes and before I know it, I'm sitting at my desk again, tappity tapping away like the weekend never even happened and is just a distant memory of someone living their best life, or ya know spending all weekend watching Netflix in your PJs.

First of all, who made the rule up of a five day working week and only a two day weekend. I bet it was a man who hated his family and wanted the excuse not to see them. I've got you pegged, sunshine.

Waking up on a Friday is just one of the best feelings in life. It's like yes, I have work, but woo, the weekend is almost here, la, la, la, nothing can get me down today. Satan, you can test me all you want, hun, but my mood cannot be taken down. Not even by Dave in accounting moaning that we've gone over budget. This has never happened to me but I bet it is totally something Dave would say. Urgh, god, Dave, give it a rest.

Sleep is one of my favourite things in life. It is just the best thing ever invented and I just *love* it. I am not a morning person, never have been, never will be. Do not wake me up before ten a.m. if you expect me to still like you. I do not take kindly to being disturbed. In fact, I will constantly moan like the little bitch that I am. You have been warned.

As you can imagine, getting up early of a morning to participate in a bit of working action is not something I want to be a part of. But ya know, these holidays and handbags won't pay for themselves. So, there you will find me when my alarm starts screeching every day, contemplating my entire life's existence and if I quit instead of getting up will I be able to maybe just buy the handbag instead.

I'm not sure why and I *will* find out, but the answer is always no. *No, Nik, you can't quit. No, Nik, you won't ever find a job that will have you jumping out of bed at six-thirty every morning with a smile on your face doing the conga to the kitchen. So get up, we must and live on to fight another day.* Such a chore.

So, whilst I lie there contemplating my whole life's existence and if I really should throw the damn alarm clock through the window, a thought comes to mind: *Woo, there's only four more days until the weekend. Yyyas, Nik, you can do this. Get your butt up and focus on four more early get ups, come on, girl. You got this.*

(Sidenote: my future husband is going to read this and divorce me immediately and I wouldn't stop him. I am incredibly hard work and an absolute menace to society. But I am funny and kinda cute so ya know.)

It was only lately that I realised, what is this life. No, seriously, do we just spend all week praying for the weekend. Then woo, yeah, Saturday, Sunday. Sunday night the Monday scaries come, and we spend our last few hours of freedom full of anxiety and crying over *Antiques Roadshow* and the thought of what another week will bring. Only to do it again and again and again until we are lucky enough to retire before we lose our bodies and minds, or for our long lost grandmother to show up and tell us we are the future queen of Genovia. I reckon the latter is definitely the safest bet.

I decided *no*! Enough is enough. I can't and will not live like this any more. I will savour each and every day and not just be huffing and puffing every morning dragging my sleepy, lazy butt out of bed. Okay, soooo I definitely will still be huffing and puffing and I have only been doing this for a week so it isn't quite fool proof yet, *but* if you can get a grip of yourself more than I can we are for sure on to something.

How to survive just living for the weekend? Try and focus on all the things that make you happy throughout the week. Even the teeny tiny things like… the sun shining or a great meeting or a day you don't hear a peep out of Dave from accounting. Gosh, that Dave, calm down, hun.

And don't come at me if you work weekends, I can't please everyone and I was you once too and yep, you guessed it, I huffed and puffed then as well. Oh I am such a delight.

Sober nights out

All dolled up, wine glass in hand full of non-alcoholic rosé, I was pregaming for my first night on the town since I stopped drinking. I knew it would be different, but I was doing everything I could to still get that pre pub buzz and to be full of life and a good time.

Turns out I can't be full of life, sober in a room full of pissed up people. I'm more sitting in the corner, sipping my mocktail trying not to yawn or look at my watch for the fifth time in the last thirty seconds kinda girl.

If you asked my work colleagues in my job before the pandemic compared to my current job, you would think they were describing two different people. Pre pandemic I was wild. I would be the first one up dancing, get everyone involved and just be the life and soul of the party. These days I am a boring old lady sitting in the corner wishing I was back home in my PJs. What is this life.

I stopped drinking to help improve my mental health but now I think it is having the opposite effect. I don't want to be that boring person sitting there, face like a slapped arse with a sprite, it just isn't who I am. I love how most people quit drinking to better their lives and there's me acting like the psychopath I am. Why can't I be that super fun person who people don't even know isn't drinking and just have a ball. I am hoping with some practice I to get to that person and I can stay my teetotal smug self. Okay, so not fully tee-total, I will partake in some alcoholic beverage action on my holidays. Even I'm not crazy enough to be sitting around the pool in the sunshine without a cocktail. Good grief.

On my first sober night out I even had a little dance. Me? Dancing? Sober? I have not done that since I was nineteen but yet there I was dancing to three songs and not buzzing off my tits. I am super proud of myself for this and highly recommend it.

Loungewear on, hot water bottle done, blanket at the ready. This is my life now and I don't ever want to leave. Please don't make me! As much as I hated being stuck in during the pandemic, I wasn't one of those rushing back out to the bar when we were allowed.

I stayed firmly in my post COVID bubble and I was pretty happy about it. The only issue I have now is I no longer know how to function in public. What do we talk about? What did we used to talk about? What do I like? What is even my name?

I don't even know how to speak to people any more. Like, what did we chat about before the COVIDS. What did I have to say? Why don't I know how to function any more? I seem to have lost all my social skills, not that I had that many to start with, I mean eww, people. I don't remember what I used to say to people or even how I used to act around them. After the initial hiya, how's things, I'm at a loss. So how can I have a chat when I am stone cold sober and you are steaming? Although you probably won't remember what I said so I could chat any random crap.

I'll just stand there staring at you not blinking. Hoping I will get abducted by an alien or something. Please, aliens, if you exist (I mean, we all know they do) now's your time to shine.

How to survive a night out sober? Have non-alcoholic Proseccos, mocktails etcetera and make sure you drink them out of a fancy glass. That shit will definitely give you a buzz. And maybe do the complete opposite of what I do and don't beat yourself up so much. No one is the same person sober as they are when drunk.

The fear/hangxiety

I'm freezing, but I must stay cold. My head is spinning, but I am staying still. My mind is blank, but I know it's full. Full of all the stupid shit I did last night, that's what it is bloody full of. Good grief.

I peep out from under my eye mask (yes I wear an eye mask to bed, are you really surprised?). I look around the room, phew, it's mine. I made it home. I check my nails, thankfully all ten still fully intact. I check my phone with one eye closed, as this is obviously going to make whatever is on the screen so much better to handle.

Flashbacks, oooh the f'in flashbacks. Why does my brain defy me this way. It's my brain, I control you, now stop with the highlight reel of a night I am for sure trying to forget.

The morning after the night before has to be one of the worst feelings. Even when you didn't drink that much or you know a hundred percent you didn't do anything to make a tit of yourself. Yet, here comes the fear… You sure, hun? Sounds like something you would do. Let's lie here for the next hour and go over every single detail and replay every single scenario. Because I know you, and making a tit of yourself is high up there even when you're sober. First of all, rude! Second of all, you are soooo right, brain. Let's go back to sleep, ignore the outside world and hope that no one remembers your name in the next few hours, let alone that you went out last night.

Nine times out of ten my brain is wrong but that one time, oooof, that one time when the flashbacks just smack you in the face like a wet fish trying to jump out of the net to freedom, and they just keep on coming. Boom! You fell over. Boom! You tipped your drink on that fitty. Boom! You threw up all over yourself and will probably be banned for life from that bar.

Our brains are wondrous things but please shut the fuck up, hun. I know what I did and it wasn't pretty. Now bore off and let me wallow in self-pity and text my bestie to see if she still loves me. (Always yes, obviously.)

My toxic drunk trait is texting stupid men who I really shouldn't be as they are dicks and should not even be entering my head space let alone the space on my phone. *But* listen up, ladies, I have a trick, I always and I mean always delete the texts once I have sent them. That way when I wake up, there is no suspicious phone activity, texts? What texts? I also highly recommend double parking. That way your hands are always full of drinks so you have no place to even hold your phone. I am a genius, I know.

Sober Nikki really cannot cope with drunk Nikki's actions. Drunk Nikki knows sober Nikki will not wish to pick up the pieces and therefore, damage control must happen during the dark hours. It's just the law.

Well, aren't they still on the dude's phone, I hear you say? Yes, yes they are, but that's not sober Nikki's problem. Sober Nikki will ignore your replies. Sober Nikki does not want to talk to you. Duh!

Bet you're not wondering why I stopped drinking for so long any more.

How to survive the fear? There really is only one solution for this. Do not, and I cannot stress this enough, do not get shitfaced like I did and let your drunken self, try to ruin your life. She is not cool. Do not befriend her. Seriously though, it will pass in a few hours/days/weeks. Depends how much of a tit you actually were. Just ride the wave, babes, and try and jump off back into the ocean as soon as you can. Totally a metaphor, by the way, huns. No drowning on my watch. Plus, it is never as bad as our stupid brains make us think it is any ways. Right? *Right*?

Cancelling plans

Cancelling plans can go one of two ways. You can be completely relieved as you couldn't be bothered to get dressed and made up to go anyways. Or you are really, really gutted, and will be in competition with me for the whiniest bitch prize.

I completely understand that sometimes plans change and I get it as long as it is done at least a couple of hours before. If I am all dolled up and you cancel our plans, I will be so fuming you'd better run and hide.

Most of the time these days I am the relieved one. Even if I want to see the person and have been excited about it, the outside world after three p.m. just isn't for me, huns.

I am sometimes in the weird limbo land of okay, I am pretty glad these plans have been cancelled but I was also kind of looking forward to it and now I am all confused about how to feel. I was also very much looking forward to the food we would be consuming. Now what am I going to have for dinner. Rude!

I didn't even have a clue what to wear and we all know me and my family pack sausages would have had a right mare getting ready so there is that. Jokes on them for cancelling really, as I probably would be doing the same after screaming into my wardrobe for a good hour. That's it I'm not going. Sometimes I feel that annoying green dude from that class Christmas film is my soul sister. We have so many things in common it's like we were separated at birth. We both hate people, eat our feelings and both have green hair covering our bodies. I am totally joking about one of those, I will let you decide which.

I dated this guy when I was nineteen and he cancelled on me like three times when I was full on ready to go out. Why did you let it get to three times, I hear you ask. W-w-w-wel, that is because I was stupid and young and thought that if I gave him another chance he couldn't possibly do this to me again. Turned out he was cheating on me. Why he couldn't have cancelled our plans earlier, I don't know. Oh boy, was I stupid and dumb. (Read, still am, please refer to the dating chapter #hahahasendhelp.)

On the flip side, you could be the one doing the cancelling. I am not one for last minute cancellations unless there has been an emergency. I had to cancel plans before as I fell down the stairs whilst getting ready for said plans. Few hours and an x-ray later and I had my leg in plaster up to my knee. If a broken foot is not an approved reason to cancel, I don't know what is.

How to survive someone cancelling plans? Cut them out of your life and never speak with them again. Just kidding, unless they play you for a fool like that guy did to me, then snip, snip, huns. How to survive wanting to cancel plans? Just be honest. We all have a period of not feeling it sometimes.

Overthinking

If there was an award for overthinking, I would win it every damn time. My overthinking constantly has me spiralling and down a path that I cannot stop. Even when I am aware of what's happening and try to talk myself out of it, my brain is like yes, Nik, but are you sure we are just overthinking or is it something we should definitely be overthinking about. You know what brain? I think you're right. (Me screaming internally nooooo, you're not!)

When your brain defies you it is just the worst and quite frankly very rude and an absolute cheek. Like, umm hello, I look after you. I read, I watch documentaries (sometimes), I have intelligent conversations (again sometimes). My brain could at least have the audacity to be kind to me rather than try to repeatedly screw me over and over.

I was on a fabulous weekend away a few years ago, and whilst thankfully my brain and overthinking subsided so I was able to actually go on the trip, when we were there things took a turn. I did the typical thing of thinking everyone was mad and pissed off at me.

Story time…

We were away having a lovely time. Laughs were shared, drinks were drunk, chats were had. We were stopping for a quick snack before heading back to the hotel to get ready for the evening when there was some weird activity and everyone started acting really strange and standoffish. Long story short, there was some sort of mix up with my food and it took ages to come out, and I mean ages. One group of us had gone back to the hotel before it even came out. So I automatically thought this was why everyone went weird.

If you suffer with anxiety and overthinking you will know exactly what I am talking about when I say, everyone is mad because of me. It's all my fault.

So me and my stupid brain went back to the hotel and had a little cry. I didn't feel like I could talk to anyone about it as I didn't want to be that person bringing the mood down (again, overthinking). Plus we were there for a celebration and I didn't want to be the one to bother anyone about it (yep, overthinking). I wanted to go home but was stuck so I decided to slap a smile on my face and get on with the night. After a few drinks, I had such a good night. Danced for hours and laughed with my bestie.

It wasn't until a few months later when I was casually chatting to a friend about it that I discovered the truth. It wasn't about me at all. No one was mad at me, not even a teeny tiny bit. I had pissed off absolutely no one and was left crying for no reason other than my stupid brain.

I was so mad at myself that I didn't speak up and so soooo mad that I let my brain trick me into thinking this and it ruined part of a great weekend.

Forget teaching algebra in school, they need to start having weekly lessons on not just mindfulness but anxiety, depression and how it can affect your mind so badly. They need to offer coping mechanisms and ways to trick your brain right back into thinking rationally.

How to survive overthinking? Speak up and speak out. Pull a friend or family member to the side to debrief the reasons you are feeling this way. Having an outsider listening in on your concerns can really help with overthinking. I also think saying it out loud really helps you to process it. Okay, so I'm feeling a type of away about xyz, I know it isn't a big deal but I can't shake this feeling. And know we aren't bothering someone if we do that. They are friends and should be there for you and if they aren't well they can just fuck off can't they.

Sunday scaries

Did you ever get that feeling the night before a new term or year at school where you'd been so used to being off that you just want to keep yourself to yourself? Not really speak to anyone or share your fabulous new gel pens and stay in your protective home bubble? I still get that feeling now, minus the gel pens. (Why did we ever stop buying those delightful things?)

Now being the grownup that I am, I sometimes get it the night before work. Mainly when I've been on leave or sometimes when I've only been off for the weekend. I feel like I just want my mama and I want to curl up in my duvet all day and watch films. I feel like I need the protection that home gives me.

Just like at school, as soon as I've been at work for a few minutes those feelings go away. I mean I'd still rather be at home snuggled up watching films but I'm okay that I'm not for a while (I think).

I hate the way my brain makes me feel, like excuse me, hun, it's my brain, you make me feel how I tell you to, thank you very much. Haven't we had this conversation a million times? What are you not getting?

Anxiety has a strange way of telling you you're failing at life when nothing has changed. Life was the same as yesterday or last week when you were doing great. But today, oh no, your anxiety is very suspicious of today and you should be on edge all day ready for the unexpected. Ready for your world to come crashing down because duh, why would it all be rainbows and butterflies for you.

I can't believe Sunday scaries are still a thing. It's so rude and I want no part in it.

I know I'll be okay when Monday comes around, and will be sharing my gel pens with everyone (virtually, of course, as I work from home) which makes this feeling even more ridiculous. Like, come Monday morning I am technically still in my home bubble. I may not be watching films but I can still be all cosy and protected. No one can see me or pop in my home office to ask me an annoying question. Dave and Steve can't come from whatever department I created for them and nag me about stupid shit. God, when will those guys give it a rest.

My current job (at time of print, ha, I've always wanted to say that) doesn't make me feel quite so bad and I only have to give myself a teeny pep talk now and again.

Gel pens aside, I know I've got this. But sometimes I just wish I didn't need to give myself a pep talk and I just had it, ya know?

How to survive the Sunday scaries? Take time to chill and do something that makes you happy and calm. Know that come Monday at 9.05 a.m. you will be completely fine and forget you were ever feeling this way. I tried sleep tea once, sucked for me but it could be just what you are looking for. You are welcome, huns.

Not running away from life

Fight or flight? I don't know about you, huns, but any minor inconvenience and I am off. Toodle-ooo, ta-ra, Bon voyage and all that jazz.

I am a firm believer in putting my positive pants on and dealing with whatever is thrown at me but in reality, my positive pants are in the wash, and I just want to run away, quit, move to Australia, and never return.

When anything goes slightly wrong in my life my first reaction is always nnnnah, F this, I'm not doing it any more, babes. It can be something going wrong in a job or even something as simple as a night out planned.

Something very minor happened in a job and I was like nope, this is not for me, I can't do it, I won't do it, I need to quit. After I got a grip of myself and remembered I actually really liked this job and I can do it, I did do it and did it pretty damn well. I think about quitting a job every time something goes wrong or any time someone pisses me off, and I have done so with pretty much all of my jobs. I ain't no quitter, but yeah, I think I'll quit. Ta-ra, huns.

The whole jump on a plane and run away to a faraway land does sound appealing several times a day. But unless they just let me live like a queen, sitting on the beach sipping cocktails all day, then I am probably going to be met with the same issues. Although, six months at The Atlantis in the Bahamas could very well work. I will not say no to that.

I really need to train my brain into not wanting to bail the teeny tiny split second something mildly inconveniences me. I need to have more faith in myself and realise I can do these things and I can do them well. And not wanting to leg it like Forrest Gump on his good day.

How to survive wanting to run away to Australia? Take a deep breath. Remember who the fuck you are and make it happen! I mean make happen whatever it is making you want to run away. Don't actually run away, that is terrible advice #hahahasendhelp.

Letting go

Staring at the bottle of Fanta on my bedside table, I knew I had a problem. No, it wasn't secretly filled with vodka. It had been there for twenty-nine days. Twenty-nine whole days just sitting there minding its own business with only a teeny drop left inside.

What is my problem, I hear you ask, probably out loud as you are super engrossed in this read. I've realised lately I can't seem to let it go or rather I worry about letting go of something that I can't have again.

You see, I bought said bottle of Fanta on my way home from Heathrow Airport after my fabulous New York trip and if I throw it away it means that New York is over. Every time I look at the bottle I smile and think of the trip. It's not even like I didn't bring home a suitcase full of New York branded goodies. You bet your arse I did. Everything from an Empire State Building glass to an NYC pencil.

I know that sounds crazy but I've realised lately that I do it with so many things. It's almost like I'm afraid of something being the last time.

On a summer holiday abroad, when it's the last time being in the pool I just don't want to get out. I sit there, bobbing about trying to savour every last drop.

Whenever I am somewhere with say, an amazing view, I don't want to stop looking at it because I know there will come a time when that look will be the last. It doesn't even have to be anywhere incredible. I even do it at a local beach forty minutes from my house that I have been to loads of times.

One Christmas I even had to get Carol to let me know what number of Christmas kitchen roll we were on just in case it was the last one and I hadn't prepared myself for it to be the end. Holy crap, I need to get a grip of my life. I should definitely use the money from sales of this book to see a therapist. Wonder if they have Christmas kitchen roll…

I was chatting about it to Carol who naturally suddenly became a psychologist and thought it may be something to do with losing my dad. And that the last time I did xyz with him I didn't know it was the last time. Now I have a fear that whenever I'm enjoying something that when I walk away, it could be the last time.

I don't mean that in a something is going to happen to me way. I think I'm scared of losing something, anything that I love, enjoy or is making me happy.

Maybe it's just teaching me to savour every moment more, who knows, but it's crazy to think how things have impacted your life without you even realising.

Or maybe I am now realising, as I'm writing this, that I'm scared that you don't know when everything could just end. Even that Christmas kitchen roll.

How to survive letting something go: just maybe don't? If it works for you, toss that Fanta bottle and if not, where is the harm in holding on to it for just a little longer. *Or* a healthier option (maybe, possibly, probably), savour every great moment that makes you happy. No matter how small or insignificant it may seem to others. Savour it, and know more amazingly happy moments are on their way so it is okay to say goodbye to this one.

A kid's party when you don't have kids

Aw, your little angel is turning two, that is lovely, Helen. (I literally do not have any friends call Helen so we are all safe here. If I have made friends with a Helen since time of writing, this is not about you, babes, and I am sure we are cool.) So nice for you, Helen, but you can take that invite straight back where you got it from. There is no need for an official rsvp, my face is more than enough. Thank you and goodbye.

I mean, come on, who actually enjoys these things? Even if it's my bestie's kid's birthday who I genuinely truly adore, I still don't want to come. I can adore them from afar and not at their party with some random friends of theirs coming up to me and handing me a very soggy sausage roll. The disgrace!

The only time I have actually enjoyed a kid's party has been when it was my niece or nephew. And even then it can piss me right off. Can't we just have a party with just them and no other germy kids crying and moaning about the place? If my babies moan I can give them a stern talking to. Can't do that with Helen's kids, can we, no. Because Helen will be spitting feathers and will report you to child services. Damn it, Helen!

I spent one of my nephew's parties on my hands and knees for the first hour. No, it wasn't a party that had taken a terrible turn. I was hungover to shit, hugging the toilet, throwing up every ten minutes and trying not to pee myself in the process. It was a dark time and I appreciate your thoughts and prayers. I struggled on to celebrate my little monkey, but I would not be doing that for Helen's kid. Helen's kid can kiss my arse.

And don't even get my started on a kid's party when they do not cater for adults at the buffet. You've dragged me here against my will and you now have the audacity to not feed me? I am partial to a chicken goujon and a mini pizza too, thank you very much. And yes, please throw in a cupcake for good measure.

For those reading this who do not cater for adults. I said what I said and yes, you should feel ashamed. It is the same way I felt when I had to fight my niece for a sneaky cocktail sausage because you had only catered for two per child. Grow up, will you!

A kid's party when you don't have any children is like sticking your head in a microwave while a clown is trying to fill your pants with ice. I don't want to participate in any of it. It's not funny. It's not cute. Please don't invite me.

I am at the age where I cannot be somewhere I do not want to be and sit there smiling like the Cheshire cat and pretend I give a damn when Cindy is telling me her son James can now clap and count to one. Cindy, hun, please just no.

Absolutely no disrespect to the mamas or papas who are putting on a lovely shindig for their babies. I completely get it. You should pull out all the stops and do whatever you want but I don't have to attend. I will smile at the photos you post on social from afar and send a gift in the mail.

How to survive a kid's party without kids? If you really must attend just smile and wave, boys, smile and wave. And maybe have a flask of vodka in your bag. *Just kidding*!

A kid's party when you do have kids…

Still no! Unless it's your child, this shit is just not fun.

As we have gathered I do not have or ever want children, but those who have, I know you do not enjoy going to little Bertie's fifth birthday party. Having to sit with all the bitchy mamas talking about how much better their kids are than Susie's down the road. Aw, poor Susie love, I bet little Sammy is great at catch don't worry, hun. Haters gonna hate.

I challenge you to find more than five people who actually like attending kids' parties and if you do I can pretty much guarantee they are lying.

How to survive a kids party when you do have kids? Remember, you don't have to go to every party your kids is invited to. When you are there, focus on your own kid and Susan's kid and his snotty nose can get fucked.

Someone asking when you are having kids

I have a whole new appreciation for sunglasses, because if I wasn't wearing mine right now there would be a right kick off. Sunglasses will hide a multitude of sins. Didn't get much sleep last night? Whack those sunnies on. Have an eyebrow crisis? Dig out the sunnies. On your tenth eyeroll during a three minute conversation? Praise Jesus, hallelujah for sunglasses.

I roll my eyes so much I am surprised I can actually see. I even let out a little pissed off groan sometimes just for extra effect. But when it comes to a conversation about when I am having kids, my groan is silenced yet my eyerolls are on another level.

First of all, Karen, hun, it is none of your business. Yes, I know I am in my mid-thirties and my clock is ticking. But do you know what, hun? I don't ever want children so my clock can just tick, tick, the fuck off. What's that? No, I won't change my mind when I meet someone. Why, you ask? Because as you just pointed out I am in my mid-thirties and I am pretty sure by now my feelings on this are solid and your input will make zero difference.

I may start bursting into tears and walking away so they feel really bad for asking and can mind their own business and stay back in their box next time.

I am super lucky that I don't actually want any of those germ filled delights. Given my age (thanks, Karen, hun) and the fact I am single, wanting kids would probably be tough and I do feel for those who want them and can't. Which is why you should never ask that question. God, Karen!

The life of a mother is just not for me and I am not sorry about it in the slightest. What I am sorry about is that you feel the need to be so involved in my decision to continue with the human race. You don't want to see a mini version of me, I can assure you, huns. My niece has a little of my personality and she is a handful.

Whenever I tell someone I don't want them they always give me that pity look and I find myself reassuring them that it's fine. When it totally is fine. What would not be fine was if I were to actually be pregnant or have children. Thank god we carry them. Imagine me having a child turning up at my door saying I'm their mama. No thanks, hun, off you pop. No scary door action for me, thank you very much.

The 'oh but when you meet someone you'll feel different' really gets to me. I'm going to start saying that when people say they want kids or are pregnant. Don't worry, hun, you might change your mind or if not there's always adoption.

It is always the ones with kids that are right little fuckers. The fact that your oldest kid is screaming because he wants an ice cream and the other one is licking the floor is not going to tug on my ovaries and make me run to the next man I see and beg him to impregnate me. What a lucky guy though, eh?

This also goes for asking someone who already has kids when they are having more. Isn't the world overpopulated enough? Don't we have enough people to provide for? Get back in your box, Sally, hun, and you might notice that your boy kid has done a runner and is halfway up the street. Not such a role model for mothers now, are you, Sally.

How to survive someone asking when you are having kids? Either burst into tears and run away screaming noooooo, why, God, why. Or tell them it is none of their business and be on your merry way.

Being a straight talking, opinionated, delightful human being
(Buckle up, huns, as you are in for a wild ride)

If you have got this far into the book and haven't realised how opinionated I am, then I recommend you go back to the start and go again. My delightful, opinionated personality is what makes me, me, and it is very welcomed by many until, well until it isn't.

People think opinionated and straight talking people are great to take shopping, to deal with a stressful confrontation they aren't able to or for advice they want to hear.

I am often the go to girl for a shopping trip as I always give my honest opinion and would never let anyone buy anything that didn't suit them, was too expensive for them at the time or if they just looked like a potato. Even when I owned a jewellery and accessories shop, I did not let anyone leave with anything that wasn't right for them. (Maybe that's where I went wrong. I should just have made the sale and kept my mouth shut. But that's not me, much to Carol's absolute delight.)

If something isn't right I will say it, whether that's yelling at something on the TV or confronting my boss about the way something has gone down. (I do not recommend the latter, especially if your boss is a dick as you will probably end up being fired.)

I pride myself on being open and honest. People love it when it suits them and don't when it's something they don't want to hear. 'Sure, yes. Please give me your honest opinion on the story I just told you about what my husband did.' Under no circumstances in this situation do you speak freely. Bite that tongue until you no longer have the ability to enjoy an ice cream. Being asked to give your honest opinion does not mean give your honest opinion. It means give the opinion I want you to give and if you don't I am going to give you a look so cold it could fix the polar ice caps.

Being a straight talker, I was always the one at school to get asked to help out if friends were in a tricky situation. I would always stand up for others and always spoke out when I believed something wasn't right.

I mean, what would our lives be as women if people hadn't spoken up and had an opinion.

How to survive being straight talking and opinionated? Keep doing you, hun. More people need to fight for what is right and speak up when something isn't. Don't let the bastards get you down. Haters gonna hate. Just try not to get yourself fired like I did. Whoops.

Lack of patience

As I make my way to the till point, arms loaded up with new goodies to purchase, doing my little happy shopping dance (literally consists of a little wiggle whilst beaming like a kid in a toy shop), I glance up. There are about ten people queuing in front of me and only one person on the tills.

I take a look at all the delightful treats I have just spent thirty minutes choosing. Do I really need this pink, fluffy glitter eye mask? Yes! What about the ten pack of pencils which I have a ton of at home but not like these ones, these ones have gems and sparkles on them. Yep, need these. Okay, so what about this candle. Smells of coconut, which is my fave. Sold! Say no more. Better put all these back then as I am not waiting in this queue for longer than five minutes.

Okay. Right. Okay, so looks like on this occasion we will have to just wait. Hmm, not sure about this one so I will of course moan and mumble to myself that I am hot and can't wait to get out of there. We could use this time to decide if we really need all the things we are carrying. I will assess very carefully. Should I put something back? No. Will I put that glitter flamingo back though? Also no, the hell I will.

So, the moral of the story here, guys, sometimes you just have to suck it up and buy all the crazy shit you want and wait. I know, I know, it is the absolute worst. But if you really want that fluffy notebook and matching pen, you're just going to have to do it. Be strong.

If I only have one item in my hands and there is a huge line, chances are it's going back. I will then continue to have non buying regret for about a week or so until I forget all about that glitter water bottle holder. Another note to add for my future therapist, 'a whingy little bitch who has a shopping addiction'. They are going to totally love me, even if it is just for all the money they will make from me.

Sidenote, I genuinely believe everyone should have a therapist of some kind. We all need to talk through some shit at some point and have a non-biased opinion on it. Just a little thinking out loud for you there, huns. You are welcome.

My lack of patience doesn't just stop at waiting in lines. Oh no, no, no, I am fully dedicated to my non-existent patience. I want everything I want in life and I want it now. Don't get me mixed up with Veruca Salt from *Charlie and the Chocolate Factory*. I am an absolute delight, but internally I am screaming and frustrated that it isn't happening now.

Like this book for instance, I am having the best time writing it, but I want to fast forward to holding the finished printed book in my hands. Then be choosing my outfit for the launch party. (Hell yes, there will be a launch party and I am having a Kate Spade dress vision for it.) It's not that I don't want to put in the work, I just like to see the rewards also. I know, I know, I am an absolute nightmare, *but* a delightful nightmare.

I love the build-up to a holiday. Planning and buying all your outfits, putting together an itinerary (I am the queen of an itinerary), deciding what time you should leave for the airport (seven hours before your flight, duh). It is just the best, but here I go again, once all that has happened, you've bought everything, planned everything, researched the menus at the airport, what now?

I just have to sit here like some kind of fool and wait however many weeks are left until I can have some other holiday related fun. How very dare you. Now my patience is wearing thin and I want it to happen now, please. I will close my eyes and when I open them I will be on my way to the airport. One, two, three. *Damn it*! What kind of sick joke is this?

If I have an end goal my patience isn't as bad. Still a moaning cow but a delightful moaning cow. For instance, if I have to wait in line for something or if I am waiting on something and they give me a time frame I am all good. Thirty minutes you say? Cool, I can do that. What I cannot and simply will not do is sit there for hours with no updates, no one checking in and me wondering if this is my life now, just sitting here waiting on someone else.

Can you imagine how much of a joy I am in a hospital A&E, ha, ha. Totally appreciate that they are super busy but *please* give me an accurate time frame, I beg you. Do not make me wait here, then there, then here again for hours and hours and hours without giving me any updates.

If I have to sit here for three hours, not great, but please tell me. For the love of god, *tell me*!

Whenever I go to the doctors' I always ask how many people are in front of me or if they are running late. I have learnt from my mistakes of sitting there for ten years thinking my name is going to be called next and there's another hundred people in front of me.

Carol says I get it from my dad, he hated to wait too, so really it's not my fault, he made me, it's his fault. Sorry, Rob!

Walk into a restaurant, 'Ah sorry it is a two hour wait.' The hell it is, hun. I am off, babes, not happening here. And we all know it will probably not just be two hours and I for one will not be sticking around to find out. Ta-ra, hun, ta-ra.

So, you know the drill, huns, don't make me wait to read this book. Buy it. Read it. Love it. Thems the rules.

How to survive lack of patience? Do not listen to me. I have no tips here. If you do, please send them my way. I suck at this and probably always will. Do I care? Not sure I have the patience to think about it. Now where did I put that sequin flamingo?

Not reacting

I wanted to call this chapter, 'Trying to remain calm and not go ape shit and losing your mind in a heightened situation', but I felt it didn't quite have a good ring to it and was a little long.

When I lose my head, I like to shout. It's not that I am angry, I am just loud. When people keep pushing your buttons and are waiting for you to react, I wish I could just sit there smiling and not give into their childish desires. Instead, I go from zero to a hundred like I'm trying to win some sort of cash prize.

Every time this happens, I always get so annoyed with myself and vow to never act like that again. But I do act like that again and then I regret it once more. It's just a vicious circle of never-ending stupidity.

My parents always used to say that whenever you shout and screech you lose the argument. They are so right, yet here I am trying to get my opinion across and being very loud in the process as that's the only way, right?

The only person I tend to lose my head with is my sister. Ah, siblings, they have your back but know how to push your buttons. They would kill for you but will also try to kill you. Thems the rules.

We are a super close family but ooof, she knows how to set me off. Sometimes she has this look in her eye and a tone of voice that I just know what's coming. Trying not to slap your sibling about a bit is super hard and there should be some sort of manual for it. Tips on what is the best angle to have the most impact. I joke, I joke, I meant more of a what to do when your sibling does xyz so you don't end up in jail. I'm sure this works both ways. I am also a nightmare at times, as you've probably gathered by now.

I also get what I like to call super passionate when I see something in the news that is ridiculous. Carol calls it ranting, I call it being passionate about something that needs to change. Like when I see something on social media, or an idiot in the street. I need to release my feelings on it and a lot of the time it will be loud. Soz..

I don't know about you, huns, but I have a tendency of shouting near people about something. I'm like, calm down, babes. I am not shouting at you, I am shouting *near* you. Big difference. Now shut your face before I bitch slap you. Totally kidding about the slapping. I don't think I have ever hit or punched anyone in my life. I will have a think about this and get back to you, but I am pretty sure I haven't. I'm not into violence. I am just into shouting to get my point across. If you just listened to me I wouldn't have to be so loud now, would I.

How to survive not reacting? I have literally no idea, huns. If you aren't some sort of psychopath like me, please let me in on your secret.

The weather

This is the life. The sun is shining. The sea is glistening. What more could I ask for of an afternoon? Umm, wait. What the hell is that? What is happening? Why is my hair wet and looking like I've been living in a bush for three days? What is this wet stuff falling from the sky? In St Lucia they call it liquid sun and I am so here for that. But rain in the Caribbean is very different to UK rain. UK rain just sucks.

Here it will rain for about forty-two years once it starts and that rain will be so heavy, we all now live underwater (Busted predicted that shit!) and no I am not overreacting in the slightest.

Our winters are cold and wet; our summers are warm and wet with a week or so of a heatwave where we all bitch and moan that it's too hot and we can't wait for the winter to come. Then the winter comes and we are freezing our arses off, wishing we had a second home in the Maldives. It's just a vicious circle.

UK weather has us planning summer day trips ten minutes before we pack up the car and leave. Even then, by the time you reach your destination the weather has probably taken a turn and you now have to go back home again.

It is April as I am writing this and I am sitting here with a blanket and hot water bottle and am still shivering my titties off. But give it thirty minutes and my titties will be out as it will be too hot. (Just kidding, ain't nobody want to see these bad boys out in all their glory.)

When we have a super sunny day, so many people are like see, you don't need to go abroad when we have this weather. Yes, okay, Karen, it is lovely now, yes agreed, but can we guarantee I can sit here in my pool on my lilo for the next week to ten days being plied with cocktails? I don't think so, hun. I don't actually have a pool, it's a paddling pool, okay, but boy does it bring me joy during those ten minutes of sunshine.

How to survive Great British weather? Layers, layer and more layers. Also, take a huge bag big enough to fit your sunglasses, umbrella, winter hat, summer hat, gloves, scarf, jumper, coat and a beach kaftan. Sorted.

Holidays

How to survive a holiday? Before you think I have completely lost the plot to the point of no return, hear me out.

The moment we step out of that plane is one of the best feelings in the world. The heat slaps you in the face like a warm hug from the sunshine itself, and the holiday smells just fill you with so much glee you could pee a little. Where's my potty?

The build-up to the holiday is super exciting. The planning, the packing, the shopping trips. Oh, I am getting goosebumps just thinking about it.

Where do my epic survival tips come in to play? Well, I am glad you asked, Sharon. There are sooo many shitty and stressful parts to going on a holiday that we could all do with a helping hand.

Let me break them down for you:

Trying to fit everything in your suitcase

No, I will not take out the five extra outfits I packed or my pillow so we can do the case up easier. Good grief, who do you think I am?

Finding out your passport has expired when you leave in three days

Me one Thursday evening: 'Yay, we've just booked a holiday. We leave Sunday.'

Carol: 'How exciting. Can't wait. Oh, I'd better check my passport. I'm sure it's fine.'

Narrator: But it was not fine. It was not fine at all. Carol's passport had run out and now Nikki was going to have to disown her and find a new mum to take.

True story and one I do not wish to ever relive. Thankfully a quick trip to the Passport Office (for my dad whilst we were at work), several hours waiting and we were good to go with a brand new passport for Carol. Woo.

Getting to the airport

Do I leave way more than enough time to get there and risk being bored hanging around on the world's most uncomfortable chairs? Or do I leave in just enough time and hope to all the gods that ever lived that we hit zero traffic and breeze through every green light? Do we need to book a hotel the night before? What time do I need to get up to make sure I leave on time? It's just all too much for me, but I love it.

Checking in

Is my bag going to weigh too much and I will be charged almost the same price of my holiday to just put the same case on the same plane being carried by the same people? Where even do the excess luggage charges go?

Security

Okay, Nik. Stay calm. We will be fine. If we get searched it will be super-fast and they won't find anything. Yes, but what if I accidently packed a gun I do not own, or what if someone threw a bag of drugs into my handbag when I wasn't looking. Or they could have made me swallow some or shoved it up my arse and I had completely forgotten. Or what if I was part of a money laundering ring I forgot about and have a bunch of cash stuffed in my backpack with no reasonable answer as to why it is there?

Airport departure lounge

Ah, the best part. Pass me my pint. (We do not care that it is only six a.m. Time doesn't exist at the airport.) Those eighteen months of not drinking were terrible. Yeah, sure I'll buy some overpriced snacks. Why the hell not, I'm on my holidays. Magazine that I won't read and will come all the way to my destination and back again? Sure, get it in my bag, hun. Oh, but I can't see the screen here with all the gate numbers. Shall we move? Ah, but I want to press my face up against the window and watch the planes landing. Okay, why don't we take it in turns to keep running back and forth to glare up at the screen every fifteen seconds?

Boarding

What if someone is sitting in my prebooked seat? I'll just politely ask them to move, it will be fine. They will totally understand and be more than happy to accommodate me. Oh Christ, there is someone sitting in my window seat. She is staring at me like she has zero intentions of moving. Do I call the pilot? I feel like he/she would really want to know about this. This actually happened on a flight to or maybe from Greece. This woman just looked at me happy as Larry, sitting in *my* window seat. *My* window seat and had the audacity to look at me like I was the bitch because I wanted her to move. The flight attendant said it was fine and we didn't have to switch. Um, I'll tell you what is fine when it comes to the seat I paid extra for thanks hun, and this isn't fine in the slightest.

Plane Seats

Now I'm five foot nine so I like to prebook extra legroom. The length of my leg from knee to my hip is very long, so to avoid wearing my legs as a necklace I am all about the extra legroom or extra space seats. You get a lovely seat in an emergency exit aisle. Perfect, all comfy, ready to go. Then they come over and give you all these rules and info to read. So basically I am now in charge of everyone on this plane should there be a crash. Your lives are literally in my hands, huns, and I'm not sure I am up for the responsibility.

First of all I am barely responsible for myself, never mind a plane full of people. Second of all, I will be the first one out that door, praying to all the gods on my way down the slide shoot. You really don't want me in charge of anyone's life, but I would quite like this extra legroom, thank you very much. Torn between wanting comfort (well, as comfortable as you can get on a plane these days) and wondering if I should just sack it off and go and sit stress free somewhere else. *But* then I glance at who is in charge on the other side of the plane and I feel like I am way more equipped to handle this than they seem to be. Especially since they are now pretending to open the exit door. Please sit your arses down. I've got this!

Mile high snacks

Get your minds out of the gutter, huns, I am talking toasties here. Pure filth. I'm in seat 32 but I will just sit here with my hand firmly gripped around my money (pounds, not euros, I am not cracking into my holiday cash on the flight.

Do you think I am some kind of animal?) for the next thirty minutes until the flight attendant gets to me. Nope, can't put it down, I might miss out on the snacks altogether. The horror.

Baggage claim

Okay, stay calm, my suitcase is totally going to be the next one. Riiight. It will be coming out next, just watch. Okay, it's not here yet, but it will be. What if it isn't? What if I have to live the next seven nights in my aeroplane outfit? I mean, it was perfect for the flight, but I can't be wearing joggers and a T-shirt in the pool, for goodness sakes. Thank god I'm wearing my hat and sunnies, that would have pushed me right over the edge. Oh phew, here it is. Those three minutes were tough.

Transportation to hotel

Whether you get a bus or taxi to your hotel, finding it outside the airport can be a bloody nightmare. Plus we all know the whiney little bitch that I am will have something to say about wandering around in thirty degree heat dragging the twelve suitcases behind me as I don't know how to pack light.

Room

Oh my god, oh my god, oh my god. What's the view like? Lemme see, lemme see. Oh, it's just a car park. But it's a Greek car park, woohoo, totally different to any car park we would see in the UK. This is fabulous. Look at that car with the funny numberplate. Oh, what a wild view. Do you reckon there are any cameras in here? Like, can they see me right now? Me screaming internally as I wave to all the mirrors and lamps. Poor bastards if they could see me though. They would need therapy seeing me in all my naked glory. They would quit the camera game right there and then. You are welcome, guys.

How to survive a holiday? Don't listen to me and all my issues. Have a word with yourself, relax and enjoy. And if Karen is sitting in your plane seat, quietly ring 999 and have her escorted off the plane for being the menace to society we all know she is.

Buyer's regret

To most people, buyer's regret or remorse is down to making a purchase, often extravagant, that they really wish they did not buy. Me? I have buyer's regret for the things I do not buy. Which is why I pretty much spoil myself all the time and buy everything that I see. Who wants to go home crying because they didn't buy a snow globe on their family trip to Greece? Not me, huns, that's for sure.

I am in my element when I am shopping on my holidays. Even just typing this fills me with such excitement. (Sidenote, maybe I should see a professional after writing this book and I don't mean a personal shopper.) Shopping is my one true love and I am my best self when holding four fridge magnets and three keyrings all branded with the place I am holidaying at. Yes, they are all for me and yes, I definitely need every single one of them.

Now, don't get this confused, I am no spoilt brat, I work for my money and if I wish to spend it on a Harrods egg cup or two, why the hell not. Sidenote, I am not rich *(yet)* I just love to buy (myself) things.

I was on a thirtieth birthday trip to New York a few years ago and I woke up in a panic on our last night because I hadn't bought a framed Fashion Avenue sign.

And if you think I spent our last morning looking for said frame you would be absolutely correct. It is hanging in my bedroom as we speak and has been a background to many an Insta snap. Thank the lord and all his disciples that we had some time that morning or I would have been crying (and moaning) all the way home. Carol would have been fuming.

So now I save throughout the year so I can buy all the stupid shit I want when I go on holiday. Five Christmas tree decorations? Sure, throw them in, hun. A New York branded glasses case that doesn't fit my glasses particularly well? Damn straight. A phone case for a phone I will possibly be upgrading in two months? Hell yes, could you also gift wrap it please so it feels like a nice little treat when I open it again back at the hotel. And then again at home to show people. And then again to actually put it on my phone. (Side note, did not upgrade my phone so now who's looking like a fool. It sure as hell ain't me.)

I did sadly have a tad case of shoppers regret on that holiday, and I hate to take a dark turn with this book, and it is still hard to talk about and something that I will just have to live with forever. (Pass the tissues, hun.) Not buying an Empire State Building hoody will be something that I can never forgive myself for and something that will haunt me for the rest of my life. The pain I feel just sharing this is so intense. I mean, I did buy one in navy but I *really* wish I had bought it in the light blue too and now I will never know how good I could have looked in said hoody. Sorry, I just need to take a minute…

I know you can all feel my pain and I'd like to thank you all for your thoughts and praise during this difficult time. And fear not, huns, I will of course go back soon to get it and will probably (almost definitely) buy it in several other colours just in case. I learn from my mistakes! I ain't no fool.

How to survive buyer's regret? Buy it aaaal Buy everything. Buy it in every colour, shade, pattern, the lot. Because if you don't I will and I definitely certainly do kind of not really but do need it and want it. Disclaimer only buy what you can afford and do not go into debt. I will not and cannot be held responsible for your finances. I can barely control my own. I cannot be the reason you have lost your house and car because you just had to buy that second tea towel in Greece. I just won't do it, huns.

Christmas (with family/people you don't like)

Ah, Christmas, you absolute beautiful bastard. My favourite time of the year and one where I will be like a hyper six-year-old from about October. It fills me with so much joy I could literally burst, spraying out tinsel and glitter covering the globe. If you don't like Christmas, we can't be friends, there is no way around it.

I adore everything and anything Christmas related. Christmas jumper day? Sure, which one as I have like twelve? Secret Santa? Yes, let's get involved, I am already online shopping for the most perfect gift. Mince pie eating contest? Fuck yeah. I mean I hate mince pies but I will happily watch someone else doing it. It is just the best. I will be asking Alexa to play my Christmas playlist so often, I think even she wants to tell me to get fucked.

The only thing I do not like about it (shocking, I know), is when you have to do things with people you don't like. Yuck! Christmas is a time for joy and festive cheer and when my festive cheer is being sucked out of me by the Grinch I am not a happy Christmas elf. I mean, I am still super crazy and unbearable but not as unbearable as one would like to be.

Christmas lunch with people you highly dislike? Urgh, why, baby Jesus, why? I am trying to celebrate your birthday with a turkey feast and this is how you repay me?

As I have probably said a billion times throughout this book, having to act like you are happy in a situation you hate is soooo draining. And Christmas just isn't the time for it.

So we have several options:

- Get so drunk that we tell the Grinch exactly what we think of them and ruin Christmas for everyone. (A strong start on this option.)
  Whilst the Grinch is being their Grinchy self and killing your vibe, smile, nod and drown them out by singing Christmas tunes in your head.
- Pretend Mr Grinchy Grinch doesn't even exist and carry on having the best day ever and the Grinch can fuck the fuck off. Ta-ra, hun.
- Or, and my personal favourite, is to turn up the festivities so much that the Grinch bursts due to too much festive cheer and you never have to see him ever again.

Work Christmas parties are a fabulous time to be alive. I am always so hyped up even before I consume any alcohol so you can imagine how my Christmas nights out end up. The only issue when it comes to work parties is apparently all of the people that work there must be invited. How petty!

So yep, that means Dave in accounting who will talk about you going over budget the whole time. Susie in HR telling you that your top is too low once again. Susie, stop looking over at my titties and you wouldn't see them. And Steve in sales letting you know just how many targets he has hit this year. Steve, jog on, I couldn't give two hoots. You do not exist, please shut your face and let me be on my merry way. (None of this has ever happened to me by the way, I'm not sure where I think I work with that description, LOL, but we all know a Dave, right?)

How to survive Christmas with sucky people? You do you, hun. Christmas comes but once a year; don't let the fuckers ruin it. Grab that tinsel, deck those halls and rock around that tree.

Alexa

'I'm sorry I don't know that one.'

'Alexa, please play *my* playlist.'

'*Alexaaaa*!'

'You know, the playlist you were playing all day yesterday and the day before. Please play that one.'

'Here's a station you may like.'

'*Alexa, noooo*. Just stop.'

'Alexa, ssssstop'

Literally like living with a five-year-old who you've asked to put their socks on ten times, and they couldn't give a fuck what you think. As far as they are concerned socks do not exist.

Alexa is one of the best things that has ever happened to me. (Yes, we have established I don't get out much.) We (my sister and I) purchased one for Carol as a Christmas present one year. Oh, what joy it brought her. I mean, I had to set the whole thing up and explain how to work it but oh, did she have fun once she got going. Carol, I mean, not Alexa, although I am sure she had a ball too.

Despite the whole setting up debacle I was obsessed with this new little angel sent from heaven, and I wanted in on the action too. Cue me placing a super-fast order to Argos to purchase my very own Alexa, in pink of course.

The first few weeks were so joyful. We sang together. Laughed together. Even participated in a quiz that one day. She was just the void I was missing in life.

Just like most great things in life, it took a turn. It took a turn because the stupid pink circle of shit decided to not listen, or claim to understand what I was even saying and started saying things like 'sorry I don't have that one', when I knew full well she did because she had played it three times just a few hours ago. Good grief!

What the hell is with her when she pipes up when you haven't even said anything to her. Mind your own business, Alexa, babes. Then when you do call her, *nothing*! Sidenote, have you tried the whisper mode? That shit is creepy as!

She had gone from being my fun loving mini disco to an absolute shit show of back chat and idiocy. Now, some may say (ahem, Carol) it's my fault and I shout at her too much and I need to calm down. I say she needs to get her shit together and stop being a spoilt brat. (Alexa, not Carol.)

How to survive an Alexa? If you have kids she will be a walk in the park. A nice break, maybe, as you don't have to feed her, water her or tell her not to take her pants off and wear them on her head. For me she will be my little music box of joy that sometimes acts like a dick, and I want to throw her through the window. (Don't. Totally not worth it.)

I mean we are still cool now, but when we laugh together it just isn't the same.

Sidenote: there are many other forms of home music robots available.

Awkward conversations

I am the queen of awkward conversations and I will think about those conversations over and over for the rest of my life. Saw a friend in the park this morning. Haven't seen him for a while. Didn't know what to say to him. Looked like a right fucking numpty and now I can't stop cringing about it.

I'm worse at conversations when I am caught off guard. If I know I'm meeting someone, I am completely fine. If it creeps up on you when you're balls deep in a chocolate éclair, that shit is not fun.

Sometimes the words coming out of my mouth aren't even real words. Am I speaking English? Who knows. Do I even know how to speak English any more? Who even am I?

When a situation gets awkward my mind takes on a life of its own and now it seems to want to kill me. I could literally write a book just of all the awkward conversations I have participated in but the absolute worst has to be when someone brings up my late dad.

Picture this, there I am minding my own business. Having some lovely fresh air and some quiet time and walking towards me I see someone I know.

I see him, he sees me. We both have panic spread right across our faces. Eyes darting back and forth looking for an emergency exit. A fire door from life where you can just walk not run to safety. We both know we've seen each other yet we still look around in hopes that what is about to happen will not actually happen.

Before I know it we are standing in front of each other in complete silence. Oh okay, it's happening. 'Hiya,' I say in a tone the complete opposite of confidence.

'Hello,' I hear back. 'I'm so sorry to hear about your dad.'

'Ah, thank you, it was a bit of a shock,' I reply, with a tiny smile at the end to make sure this guy completely not related to my dad in any way feels at ease in this conversation.

O…. kay now we are just staring at each other like a shit game of who blinks first.

'Ah well, never mind, eh,' I say, completely stunned. *Never mind, ah well*! What even are those words that just came out of my mouth. Great, now I look like the psycho that doesn't care her dad's just died. Oh and now that weird smile is back. Great stuff!

Let's just edge away slowly. Maybe time will freeze and I can run away without him ever remember this conversation happening. Good grief!

This does not beat the time a new co-worker apologised for my dad's passing to which I replied, 'Ah, don't worry, you didn't kill him, did you.' Yep! I had met this person twenty-four hours ago and now I was making them wish they had killed him and been arrested so they didn't have to endure this ridiculous conversation.

Why is it that you either find yourself consoling the person, saying stupid shit, or if you're me, both.

I once had a family friend crying in my arms on Christmas Day, just three days after my dad had died. I found myself consoling him, letting him know it was all going to be okay and my dad wouldn't want him to be sad. There are a million things wrong with this picture and it is pretty laughable, thank the lord! I'm so sorry my dad has done this to you. The absolute cheek of him. There, there don't upset yourself, hun. It will all be okay. Merry Christmas.

How to survive awkward conversations? Smile and wave, boys, smile and wave. They don't know what to say. You don't know what to say. Just thank them. Say got to go, busy-busy and go on about your day. We shouldn't have to take on other people's feelings on this when we aren't really sure what we feel ourselves. All of the feels and numb at the same time makes your brain go to mush. Awkward conversations non death related? I have absolutely no idea. Please let me know as I need to make it stop. I should just put my hand over my mouth and hope for the best.

Neighbours

No, I do not mean the Australian soap that got cancelled and is now making a comeback. What an emotional rollercoaster they've had us on, I am talking about your neighbours. The ones you see every day and don't utter a word too. Ah, Julie, no, please don't make eye contact with me. I am not in the mood for you and that fucking ugly fish right now. Look away, Julie, *look away*. 'Oh hey, Julie, how's your fish, hun?'

I am lucky that I have lived in my house all my life and love most of my neighbours and would willingly sit out my front and have a chat.

Urgh, but some I just don't have time for and my face cannot pretend that I am interested. I'm sorry, I tried, my face just does what it wants. Sue me!

Most people my age don't seem to speak to their neighbours at all. There are pros and cons to this, huns. Let me fill you in.

Pros:
- They won't ask you to feed their cat or water their plants.

- You won't have to have random chit chats with them on your way in from work when all you want to do is get your PJs on and cry about your day.
- You won't have to check in on them or look after them. My next door neighbour used to just walk into my house uninvited. It used to wind me the hell up but she's dead now so there we are. She was almost a hundred, it's fine, she had a good life. I didn't kill her, by the way, felt I needed to put that out there. What was my point? Oh yes, we became so close to her that she would join us for Christmas dinner, my parents would take her shopping, she would lift the saucepan lid when we were cooking to see what was inside. (Da fuck!) This led to my parents looking after her when she wasn't able. Which was a blessing and a curse that became just a curse very quickly.

Cons:
- The only con I can think of is that if you don't speak to them or know who they are, chances are if your house is getting broken into they won't give two shits.

You have been warned. Maybe find some happy middle ground where they won't invade your hob but will kindly have a peek out of their window should you be on holidays. Thanks, Julie, hun.

'*Oh, Julie,*' I say from the protection of my own car where Julie is nowhere to be seen. 'The fuck you think you're doing parking in my space?' We don't have allocated spaces where I live but it is just common courtesy, ya know? An unspoken law. I don't park in Julie's space ever, so I expect her to have the same respect. But nooooooo, here we are, six o'clock of an evening and I have nowhere to park. Fuck sake, Julie.

I am like the parking police in my street. If everyone parked their vehicle right outside their houses we wouldn't have any problems. No, not down a little into next door's. Bang right outside your own house, it will fit your car perfectly. I don't want to hear another word on the matter. Don't be a dick, hun.

How to survive neighbours? Again not the Australian soap, that shit is fabulous. How to survive your own neighbours. Talk enough to them that they would kindly stop someone robbing your house, but not enough so they try and move in with you for a week when they have the flu. Also don't park in my space and we will be fine and dandy.

Neighbours, if you are reading this, I will let you decide which ones I don't particularly love. Is it you? Who knows! Definitely not Sandra though, she's my girl! Love you, Sand.

Stranger danger

We spend our lives teaching children not to talk to strangers. Not in the park. Not in the supermarket. Not on the train. I propose that we start teaching adults to do this also. With that, I mean, if I don't know you, please don't talk to me. Hell, don't even look at me.

Strangers are scary and the only ones I am interested in talking to is if they are offering me sweeties. Yes, sir, I will step into your van for a Haribo. Makes total sense to me. A full pack that is, I am not interacting with a stranger just for a single sweet. What am I? Stupid?

Interacting with me on public transport is a no go. Being on public transport in the first place is a no go, but needs must and if you find me on there, mind your own business and please go about your day.

It is probably early in the morning or late evening and I will not want to be bothered with train small talk. I just can't and will not do it. I am the worst morning person and I will just grunt at you and that's if you are lucky, most people will get a weird facial expression that I couldn't do on command even if I was paid to.

I am that misery with a face like a slapped butt, or its more well-known title: resting bitch face. Please allow me to go about my day without any awkward interactions. I am pulling a face just writing this. The absolute horror.

What is up with that weird smile we do when passing someone in the street. I can't even describe it. It's like a half arsed non-smile, smile. Fairly certain I look like an absolute bellend doing it which is why I try and look in the opposite direction. No, I am not rude, I am a scaredy cat.

Which is also why in the teeniest hint of sunshine I will be wearing my sunnies. There actually doesn't need to be any sunshine; as long as it is not dark or pouring with rain, my sunglasses will be permanently attached to my face. That way no one can tell where you are looking. I could be walking with my eyes closed for all they know. Soz, hun, can't see you.

I am totally that drunk person in a bar restroom chatting to everyone as if they are my BFFs. I love this for us women, we are so great.

Drunken me in bar toilet: 'Love your lipstick.'

Equally drunken stranger: 'Aw, thanks so much, want to come to my wedding?'

Me: 'Umm yeah, I wouldn't miss it for the world, bestie!'

These are the only stranger encounters I approve of when in reality we should be super wary of drunken interactions. Ha, ha, what are we like, eh?

How to survive stranger danger? Wear a badge that says 'back the fuck up, hun'. I am totally going to copyright that! Do not engage, pull an awkward smile and be on your merry way. If you don't mind stranger encounters we cannot be friends. You are the company you keep and I do not associate myself with psychopaths. Thank you!

Working on Your Goals

Having goals and dreams is something I live for. I can't stand not having anything to work towards in life or not having something amazing in life that I truly want (and no I am not just talking about the latest Kate Spade bag, I think).

For me, having dreams and goals keeps me going every day and tends to pull me out of my funk when needed. When you have something exciting going on in your life, whether it is just in the idea stage or it is actually happening, you want to scream it from the rooftops. The sad thing is when it comes to these dreams and goals a lot of people don't want to hear it. These are the people who believe they can't achieve theirs so they either don't want you to achieve yours or if they can't do it neither can you.

These dream suckers will have you doubting yourself quicker than a penguin in a panda parade. They will make you feel your idea is dumb and someone like you from somewhere like where you live will never be able to make it. I say fuck you, hun, just watch me!

Once you realise that they are just arseholes and you can do it, use them to fuel your drive and passion. When you feel like you can't spend another second after you've finished your nine to five day job typing at your computer working on what you truly want, use them to give you a kick up the arse and relight that fire in your belly.

Not to be that person, but the only person who can stop you is you. If you choose to let these people in to your head, you will drown. You need to shake it off and keep going. Negativity, fear and doubt will ruin more dreams than a shit idea ever will.

Jealousy often gets the better of people and they don't want to see even their friends win, as it can make them accountable for their own lives where they did nothing. It is such a horrible feeling when you are so excited to tell someone amazing news and their reaction is so far from the one you expected. It is sad really, but hey, we move on. Also it shows who the true people are in your life and just let the trash take itself out. Ta-ra, hun. Off you fuck.

How to survive working on your goals and dreams? Be so into what you are doing that you can't hear any outside noise. We don't got time for that. As rubbish as it is, don't share your excitement with certain people too soon. They will crush you like a bug on a windscreen. Use the negativity as a driving force and don't look back. Don't hate me cause you ain't me, honey. PS. I have written a book!

Until next time

Upon concluding the writing of this book, I have uncovered a number of things about myself. Mainly the fact that I may need professional help or maybe just need to write a second book. I mean, who am I to deprive the world of such wisdom and joy?

I wrote this book to brighten up the shitty times in our lives. I wanted to make you laugh and smile where you would usually shout and cry.

The moral of the story is…

Life is really fucking hard sometimes, huns, and sometimes we just have to get through each day as best we can. Life will be full of ups and downs, great times and horrendous times, but always remember you can handle it all.

You may feel like you can't but please believe me when I say *you can*. We must laugh at the silly little moments that want to make us scream. Even when you want to scream so loud the man on the moon can hear you and will think he's under attack. Don't worry, hun, you're safe. Even then you still got this.

We must smile at ourselves when we do stupid shit and remind ourselves it is totally acceptable to remove ourselves from a situation we feel doesn't suit. I mean, you can't go leaving work at nine-fifteen and blaming me. 'Tara, Steve. I am sick to death of your nonsense, I am out.' I take no responsibility for any firings.

I will, however, take responsibility for you taking your power back, standing up for yourself and what is right for you, and saying a big *fat no* to what isn't.

Sorry, Cindy, hun, I will not be attending little Jeffery's Christening because quite frankly I would rather go to hell myself than sit through an hour of a stranger talking about how wonderful your son is when we all know he's a little shit.

It's okay to say no. It's okay to give yourself time to consult. It's okay to live your life how you choose. (Again, within reason, you have bills to pay remember, put that middle finger down in the team meeting.)

This book is for all you amazing huns out there to know that you have a choice. Want to stick that middle finger up Dave's arse? Maybe look for another job. Sure, might be the highlight of Dave's life but it could also be a lawsuit waiting to happen. Plus, we've just had our nails done.

We don't have to do anything just because we feel we are meant to. Think of what makes you happy and strive for it. You can change your life as often as you want. It may take some time but if you want it, you got this.

Be inspired every day to live the life you want. It can literally be as simple as saying no to an invitation, spending less time on social media or even smiling at yourself in the mirror. Small changes can make a huge difference to your happiness.

You may need a little help. When our car breaks down we ask a friend for advice or get professional help. You can and should also ask when you break down. I mean don't call the mechanic, they won't be much help and will probably hang up on you, but there is always someone out there who will listen and wants to listen.

And as Carol oh ever so wisely says, 'Everything happens for a reason.' You may not know what it is at the time and it may take years before you even find said reason but trust me (and Carol), there is one.

How to survive the delightful crazy shit life throws at you? Just survive one day at a time and laugh as often as you can, as a world without laughter is not one I want to be a part of. It's a no from me, hun. Now laughter. Laughter, is a *total yes* from me, hun. And if you struggle to bring that smile back, remember I peed in a potty at the beach in the back of a Nissan. You are welcome.

Ta-ra. Love ya, huns

Nikki xx